4⁹⁰

The Prediction Book of Taromancy

The Prediction Book of

TAROMANCY

Gerald Boak

JAVELIN BOOKS
POOLE · DORSET

First published in the U.K. 1985 by Javelin Books,
Link House, West Street, Poole, Dorset, BH15 1LL.

Copyright © 1985 Gerald Boak

Distributed in the United States by
Sterling Publishing Co., Inc.,
2 Park Avenue, New York, N.Y. 10016.

British Library Cataloguing in Publication Data

Boak, Gerald
    The prediction book of taromancy.
    1. Divination
    I. Title
    133.3'24   BF1779.T3

ISBN 0 7137 1707 6

Typeset by Poole Typesetting (Wessex) Ltd.
Printed in Great Britain by Guernsey Press

Contents

List of Readings

List of Illustrations

PART I

1 A New System of Divination

Taromancy is a recently developed system of divination combining elements of astrology and the Tarot. The system can be used to advantage by anyone, for Taromancy requires no specialist knowledge or training on the part of the querent.

Taromancy provides a total of 84 oracular interpretations of events which take the form of Tarot readings. The language of the Tarot is employed to lift the veil between present and future, and the message of the reading we receive in response to our question seems often to probe far beyond our immediate concern.

We are frequently told not only how events are likely to take a particular course, but also something about the factors which have contributed to and will continue to affect the future as it unfolds. Taromancy is therefore rather more than a useful indicator to the future; it is also a helpful advisor in times of doubt or confusion.

The readings appear in answer to our questions through a simple process that selects the specific reading relevant to our query. The message we are given enables us then to perceive destiny's cloaked intent, and to proceed with greater confidence in the light of that knowledge.

Because Taromancy is derived from proven esoteric arts, it brings with it that unmistakable quality of appeal which manifests itself in any genuinely workable system. The appeal springs from the archetypal images employed, and the way in which the images speak to us from their birthplace in antiquity. For Taromancy communicates with the subconscious levels of the psyche, as it is here in the deepest strata of the universal mind that an understanding is reached of so many of life's more profound mysteries.

The system was born out of the need for a method of divination which could bridge the gap existing between the I Ching of the Far East, and the Tarot and astrology of the West.

The I Ching is a unique means of divination that supplies oracles via the random appearance of certain numbers obtained by tossing coins or casting yarrow stalks. Its simplicity of operation, and the suggestive nature of its 64 oracles, are doubtless major factors contributing to the survival of the I Ching over 40 or more centuries.

The problem for the average Westerner today is that the symbolic language of I Ching is too alien. It originates in an age and culture altogether too far removed for an easy understanding of the colourful metaphors employed.

The option for most people who wish to practice divination for themselves is to turn to astrology or the Tarot. Both require considerable study and practice before they can be used with any degree of success. This immediately puts both systems beyond the reach of the novice who seeks an instant response to a question. For straightforward simplicity of operation there have been few systems to date that could compete with the I Ching. Unfortunately, understanding the messages of the ancient though venerable oracle can be highly problematical.

The present writer had been a student of the occult for some years when it occurred to him that what was clearly needed was a new method of divination yielding answers with all the speed of the I Ching, yet possessing none of its more obvious disadvantages. A solution was found to exist in a Qabalistic glyph known as the Tree of Life.

The Qabalah is a complex system of symbolical correspondences through which the ultimate mysteries of Man and the Universe are eventually revealed. It is a vital cornerstone of Western occultism. The entire fabric of the Qabalah is summed up in the Tree of Life. It is this symbol that provided the sought-after means of unifying the most popular methods of divination of East and West into what is now called Taromancy. It combines the imagery and accuracy of astrology and the Tarot with the ease of operation of the I Ching.

2   The Tree of Life

As we have seen in the previous chapter, Taromancy is indebted for its existence to the Qabalistic Tree of Life. To enable us to understand more fully how Taromancy works, it will be helpful for us to examine briefly this intriguing Qabalistic glyph.

The Tree of Life is a centuries-old mystical symbol *(see diagram at p.33)* which represents the continuous creation of worldly matter from formless energy. This act of creation is traditionally said to take place in 10 distinct stages. Each stage is called a Sephirah (plural Sephiroth) which is a Hebrew word signifying number, emanation or sphere. These spheres or Sephiroth can be seen numbered 1 to 10 in the diagram.

The first Sephirah represents the ultimate form of Unity which existed before the fragmenting process of creation occurred. Some may regard this Unity as divine and see it as God; others may rather see it as undifferentiated consciousness, or as pure energy. Whatever the personal view preferred, the first Sephirah marks the initial stage of creation from which the remaining nine Sephiroth descend in ordered sequence.

The first three Sephiroth symbolise purely abstract states or spiritual conditions; these gradually become more 'real' until we reach the tenth and final Sephirah. This represents the entire material sphere of our mundane existence.

The Tree of Life is, in fact, an attempt to portray a highly complex chain of causes and their effects in such a way that it can be used to chart creation in both a macrocosmic and microcosmic sense. It is therefore equally a guide to the creation of the Universe as it is to a single thought originating within ourselves.

There is a very definite link between mind and matter, or Man and the Infinite, as even science will concede. To the Qabalist, this link is portrayed perfectly by the Tree of Life. It is precisely this quality of interaction between Man and the Infinite as symbolised by the Tree that fits it so ably for the purpose of divination. For the Tree of Life does not refer only to matters of the past: it is a living glyph of the present and of the ever-coming future.

Each of the 10 spheres or Sephiroth is symbolically related to one of the celestial bodies of our solar system. Thus the particular Sephirah which represents a certain fiery or energetic aspect of nature is attributed to Mars, whereas the Sephirah which represents the area of human emotions is attributed to Venus. To anyone who is familiar with the various mythologies surrounding the planets, their attributions on the Tree of Life can be seen to work very well.

The 10 Sephiroth are in turn connected by 22 individual so-called Paths. These help to portray the various stages of evolution undergone between the formation of each Sephirah. They are basically the framework of the Tree, the 'branches' which describe how the creative forces bear fruit.

Nineteenth-century occultists and scholars discovered that the essential nature of the Paths could be represented by the curious symbolism of the 22 cards of the Tarot major arcana, or trumps. The fact that there are 22* of these mysterious picture cards of unknown origin was seen to be something more than just coincidental. It was also found that 12 of the Paths could with equal justification be represented by the Signs of the Zodiac.

When these two sets of symbols were placed on the Paths, the parallels between the hidden meanings of the Signs of the Zodiac and 12 of the Tarot trumps became apparent. Henceforth, it has been recognised in occult circles that each Zodiacal Sign has its own corresponding Tarot trump. It is, however, a fact of which astrologers are sometimes ignorant.

In astrology it is held that a planet, when placed in a given Sign of the Zodiac, will produce a given effect. It will also create a similar 'effect' within the corresponding Tarot trump. This is necessarily so because the trump and Zodiacal Sign each symbolise in their own way the same basic concept. Thus Sol (or Sun) in Leo is virtually the same as saying Sol in Tarot trump XI, as the Sign of Leo corresponds with that Tarot card. The average reader however, need not be too concerned with these more technical matters.

When we say that a planet is moving into a Sign, and creating a particular effect in a Tarot trump, what we mean is that our balanced state of existence is being temporarily disturbed, that something has loomed large and, like a pebble dropped into a pond, sent its ripples across a calm surface. The Tree of Life provides a way to chart the

* There are 78 cards in a full Tarot pack; 22 major and 56 minor arcana. Modern playing cards are derived from the four suits of the minor arcana.

trajectory of the stone and the course of the ripples. It adds a whole new depth of meaning to the interpretation of events.

In Taromancy, the planets represent the influence of chance that is about to modify one's life. Each planet has its own unique nature which it imparts to the Zodiacal Sign and Tarot trump as it enters. On another level, the planet can be seen as the particular sphere of one's own Tree of Life that is currently most predominant. If the nature of the planet is in harmony with the Sign and Trump (both of which indicate one's present circumstances) the outcome should be favourable. If the planet is badly aspected the reading supplied for the event will sound a timely warning.

The interplay of planets with the Zodiacal Signs as used in Taromancy will not necessarily bear any relation to their position in the heavens at the time of the enquiry. They are universal symbols, chosen to represent the type of forces at work that will bring potentially good – or ill – fortune into our lives.

The two basic methods of using Taromancy are described in the following chapter. But briefly it may be said that the system merely requires the production of two numbers obtained by a simple process of selection, using home-made counters or dice. One number represents a Zodiacal Sign, which in turn determines the Tarot trump relevant to the situation in question. The remaining number selects one of seven planets to illustrate the dominant forces which are likely to mould the course of events. The possible permutations of 7 planets and 12 Zodiacal Signs produces the total of 84 individual readings.

A full list of the meanings of the Zodiacal Signs, Tarot trumps and planets is contained in the appendix. This will be found at the back of the book on page 119.

3 The Two Basic Methods

Each of the 84 readings opens with a short passage entitled, 'Correspondences'. This lists the various symbols that correspond Qabalistically with the two numbers which indicate that particular reading. The list is supplied to provide background information for those experienced in such matters, and may be passed over by the more casual reader.

The Correspondences are followed by the Main Principle. Under this heading we find specified the planet and Tarot trump from which the reading is derived. Here we read, Mars in Atu XIV* 'Art', or Sol in Atu IV 'The Emperor'. From this we can see which type of force (the planet) is being brought to bear on the general situation (the Tarot trump). The Zodiacal Sign itself does not form part of the Main Principle, for the Sign is subordinate to the trump. This means that the trump actually provides the reading, whereas the Sign merely tells us which trump is employed. This is not meant to denigrate astrology; it is simply that the Tarot trump can speak to us in a way which the Zodiacal Sign cannot.

After the Main Principle, from which we learn of the hidden forces at work, comes the Title of the reading. The Title is designed to encapsulate the nature of the outcome of events. It sums up and indicates the trend. Thus we see 'Stability and order' or 'Danger of stumbling'. Its purpose is to convey an instant and informing impression. We sense immediately what is in store for us.

Then follows the reading. This provides the main bulk of the answer to the querent's question. It is a detailed outline of all the elements that combine to make the reading what it is – encouraging, warning or otherwise.

The reading is written in the suggestive language of the Tarot. This means that it is picturesque: it speaks in images. We read of the Emperor

*Atu is an Egyptian word signifying 'house' or 'division' and is commonly employed in occultism as a substitute for 'Tarot trump'.

and his realm, the Lovers and their aspirations, or the journeys of the Charioteer. These Tarot characters are not to be interpreted literally. They are symbols – the phonetic script of an otherwise incomprehensible tongue. The Tarot tries to say, 'You are like an Emperor: you have trouble in your realm – the matter with which you are now concerned – and you are about to exercise your authority over it.' It is a language which is universally understood. It is not restricted by time or culture.

Though in part symbolic, the reading is clear enough in its message. The querent sees in it parallels with his or her life and circumstances that cannot be overlooked or misunderstood. The language may be picturesque, but it is far from obscure.

The readings were originally received through an occult process adopted so that the recipient's own opinions would not colour the work in hand. The intention was to produce a system of divination which could truly be said to continue the Western Mystery Tradition. The readings are thus the independent result of a method designed to meet those requirements. This is perhaps why they have such a haunting and timeless quality. Certainly, they are unlike a normal Tarot reading in the scope of their vision.

Closing each reading is a set of notes. These review the content of the reading and discuss points of interest. The notes also explain why the reading has adopted its particular outlook.

It is important when placing your question to hold in mind a firm and clear idea of what is being asked. If the mind is confused, so too will be the choice of answer received.

It is important also to frame the question so that the answer can be given without ambiguity. It would be quite useless to ask, 'Should I accept the position with Smith & Smith, or the one with Brown & Co?' Taromancy cannot be expected to choose between the alternatives. You should put the question thus; 'What would the outcome be if I accepted the position with Smith & Smith?' On receiving your reply repeat the question, but with Brown & Co in mind. Comparison of the two answers received will then allow suitable judgement to be made.

Once the information has been considered it is still up to the individual concerned how he or she then proceeds. Taromancy can do no more than indicate the probable course of events. If the signpost is ignored, one should not object when the final destination is reached.

Two methods of using Taromancy are now given. The use of either is really a matter of personal choice. It is the fixity of concentration, rather than the method, that determines success or failure.

The First Method

This involves the use of a dozen home-made counters. They can be fashioned in any form. They can be square, oblong or circular; of cardboard or any other durable and opaque material. For the sake of convenience their size ought not to exceed that of the average playing card.

Number each counter with one of the numbers in the series 1 to 12. Take care to mark the 6 and 9 so that they cannot be misread if viewed upside down.

The reverse side of the counters can be decorated if you feel that this is desirable. In which case, the more personalised the design, the better. (It is important that the design should not in any way reveal a clue to the numerical value of the counter. For this reason all 12 must be decorated in an identical manner.)

To obtain a reading, first ensure that you will remain undisturbed. Then lay out the 12 counters on a smooth surface, face upward. While concentrating hard on the question in mind, turn the counters over one by one. Then shuffle them after the manner of dominoes to ensure that they are randomly mixed. Cease shuffling when ready.

Still holding the question in mind, gather up the counters and place them in a stack, face down. Remove the top three counters. Turn the fourth counter over and note down the number it reveals.

Now turn over all the counters and remove those numbered 1, 2, 10, 11 and 12 and place them to one side. Proceed as before; turn over the seven remaining counters while concentrating on the question, shuffle, place in a stack, discard the top three and turn the fourth counter over to reveal its number. This provides the second number that you require and completes the selection process.

The first number you obtained will be between 1 and 12. Let us for an example assume that you chose the number 11. The second number you obtained will be between 3 and 9; let us here assume that you chose the number 8.

To find which reading you have been given as an answer to your question, write down the two numbers in the reverse order to which they were obtained, thus: 8 in 11.

The numbers are finally written in reverse order because the first number obtained tells us the general background to the enquiry; once this is determined we have then to discover the type of forces at work. As these forces are revealed by the second number we obtain, yet act *in* our lives, they must always be written in the sequence that portrays this effect.

In our example, the number 11 will represent the 11th Sign of the

Zodiac, with its corresponding Tarot trump, whereas 8 will represent the 8th Sephirah on the Tree of Life. Planet 8 is then the planet moving in the 11th Sign of the Zodiac, hence 8 *in* 11.

Refer to the list at the beginning of the book. There you will find that 8 in 11 refers to 'Responding to necessity' on *page 116*. Thus, 'Responding to necessity' with its descriptive reading contains the answer to your question.

The Second Method

All that is required for this method is a coin and one dice.

Step One   Throw the dice. Note whether the score is even (2, 4 or 6) or odd (1, 3 or 5) but make no further use of the actual number obtained. At this stage we merely need to determine whether the next step will be even or odd.

Step Two   If the first step was even, throw the dice twice and add together the two scores. If the first step was odd, throw the dice once only and note the score. In either case the number obtained at this stage will lie between 1 and 12.

Step Three   Throw the dice once again and note the score. Take the coin. With heads counting as two and tails counting as three, toss the coin and add the resultant score to that of the dice just thrown. This will yield a number in total between 3 and 9, and completes the selection process.

If we assume that Step Two gave us the number 7, and Step Three gave us the number 6, the two numbers would be written down in reverse order as 6 in 7. This follows the same practice as that described in the First Method of number selection. By turning to the list, we see that 6 in 7 is 'Equity and Virtue' on *page 99*. Here then, is the reading supplied in answer to our question.

It need hardly be said that one should, of course, concentrate firmly on the question in mind at the beginning of each of the three steps described above.

When you have obtained the answer to your question, do not merely read it, but allow the imagery of the language employed to communicate directly with the deeper levels of your mind. Push all your conscious thoughts to one side for a while and let the suggestive speech of the Tarot stir your intuition so that you *know*, rather than just acknowledge, the message it contains for you.

Taromancy is very much a personal matter. Only you can possibly know what the message of the reading means in relation to your own affairs. And there is no better judge of this than your own intuitive reaction to the answer you receive.

PART II

The Readings

3 in 1

Correspondences
Binah, 'Understanding'; Saturn. The Zodiacal Sign of Aries, the Ram;
Tarot Trump IV 'The Emperor'.
   Saturn rules the element Water; Aries is of Fire.

Main Principle   Saturn in Atu IV 'The Emperor'.

The Title   Improvement and progress.

The Reading

Here we observe the young Emperor who reaches a new level of ability in
the government of his Empire. Gone is the uncertainty of inexperienced
youth; the Emperor now moves with a calm and reflective majesty. This
will lead to beneficial and welcome change.

No matter how competent the Emperor has endeavoured to be in all
his past affairs, his newly found authority will bring improvement and
progress throughout the realm. The unstable will be made steady, the
weak will be made strong. All things will be appointed to their rightful
place.

In keeping with the calm and reflective manner of the Emperor,
change will come throughout his Empire in firm and unhurried degrees.
Everywhere will be seen the slow but purposeful current of improvement
and progress.

As uncertainty diminishes so does certainty increase. Therefore a
clear comprehension of rightful duty now replaces ignorance, and
encourages actions designed to fulfil the obligations of leadership. The
Emperor and his subjects will gather in the benefits of stability, order
and prosperity.

The royal advisors will observe that the seed planted long ago has matured and blossomed. Lessons have been learned. Now it is they who will receive counsel and be guided by one superior to them in knowledge.

Notes

The swift-flowing fire of newborn Aries is rigidly controlled by Saturn, which receives and refines the outpouring flame of that Cardinal Sign. Thus we see the Emperor matured and made steady. He no longer acts in short bursts of frantic activity, but proceeds with all the measured grace appropriate to one of his high position. The outcome is highly favourable.

4 in 2

Correspondences
Chesed, 'Mercy'; Jupiter. The Zodiacal Sign of Taurus, the Bull; Tarot Trump V 'the Hierophant'.
    Jupiter rules the element Water; Taurus is of Earth.

Main Principle   Jupiter in Atu V 'The Hierophant'.

The Title   Favour and assistance.

The Reading

The desire to achieve success may be pursued and fulfilled with straightforward simplicity, or through the expenditure of great effort. When great effort serves to vanquish one obstacle only to be challenged by further difficulty, it is a sign that the time is not right to pursue that path, or that the objective itself is unworthy. But when all things come together with unexpected and surprising simplicity it is a token of affirmation, a sign that both time and objective are felicitous.
    Here we observe the building up of a tower of great strength. Resources come from unexpected quarters; all things are made easy, therefore the elements are in their rightful place. The building up of the tower meets with favour throughout the family and society. A labour of aspiration now meets with unopposed success.

A creation such as a tower, when broad of base and built with precision and joy, will endure against all the forces of violence, and serve as both refuge and meeting place. It will protect and nurture. From the vantage point of its lofty elevations events will be observed at a distance; this advantage will permit the early assessment of approaching opportunity or hostility.

When resources come from unexpected quarters and intentions meet with favour and assistance, it is a time for the celebration of good fortune, and for the employment of labour in constructive deeds.

Notes

As Jupiter occupies one of the two Sephiroth between which Tarot Trump V is stationed we would expect to find things in a satisfactory state. Jupiter indicates the first appearance of form below the Abyss (the gulf between the noumenal and phenomenal) and so represents the concretion of desires. The inference is that events will materialise according to intended design.

---

5 in 3

Correspondences
Geburah, 'Strength'; Mars. the Zodiacal Sign of Gemini, the Twins; Tarot Trump VI 'The Lovers'.
Mars rules the element Fire; Gemini is of Air.

Main Principle Mars in Atu VI 'The Lovers';

The Title Discord.

The Reading

There is discord between the Lovers. Turbulent heavens boil in fury; harmony is everywhere disturbed.

The Lovers are plunged into dispute one against the other. Initial objectives are abandoned in the violent upsurge of enmity. There is a drawing apart of the once converging lines of destiny. The very Universe appears to whirl in chaos.

Light from the higher cannot now permeate the massing gloom of the lower realms. Blind anger rudely cloaks all reason.

With such discord abounding the Lovers should retire apart to tranquil places. Now is not the time to attempt union. Nor should the Lovers seek to employ the aid of sympathetic accomplices; it is far better to contain the discord than expand the influence of its effect.

In their tranquil places the Lovers will come to realise that the bringing together of two things into harmonious union is possible only when favourable potential exists. The desire for union is not in itself sufficient.

Incompatible elements may be brought together to some degree in safety, but to proceed beyond the limits of what is reasonable must result in rejection and failure.

If that rejection is accompanied by angry opposition it is clear that the initial objective of union was ill-conceived.

Notes

Mars really has no place at all in the Path of Tarot Trump VI. The aggressive, arrogant and destructive nature of Mars is counter-productive to the process that seeks to draw the Lovers towards union. Mars is 5, the Pentagram that both invokes and banishes. In Gemini, and hence in Tarot Trump VI, it banishes the forces of attraction and invokes discord. The result is failure.

6 in 4

Correspondences
Tiphareth, 'Beauty'; Sol. The Zodiacal Sign of Cancer, the Crab; Tarot Trump VII 'The Chariot'.

Sol rules the element Air; Cancer is of Water.

Main Principle   Sol in Atu VII 'The Chariot'.

The Title   Activities of consolidation.

The Reading

The Charioteer has been called to make ready for battle. In the distance can be discerned the massing forces of opposition. Dark clouds seem to span the horizon; wild beasts scurry to their sanctuaries.

There is much clamour in the preparation for battle. It is a time of fear and uncertainty. But the Charioteer must not permit himself to be

IV

ק The Emperor ♈

V

ו The Hierophant ♉

VI

ז The Lovers ♊

VII

ח The Chariot ♋

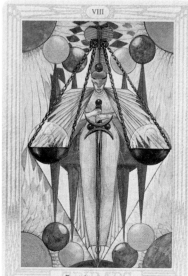

VIII · Adjustment ♎

IX · The Hermit ♍

XI · Lust ♌

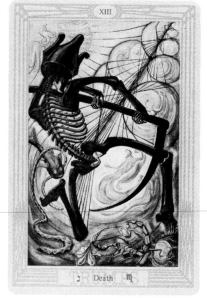

XIII · Death ♏

XIV

Recti... cando

TRUMPS — ♄ Art ♐

XV

♈ The Devil ♑

XVII

ה The Star ♒

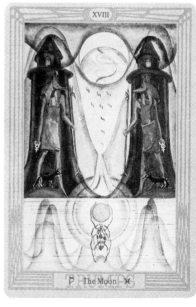

XVIII

ק The Moon ♓

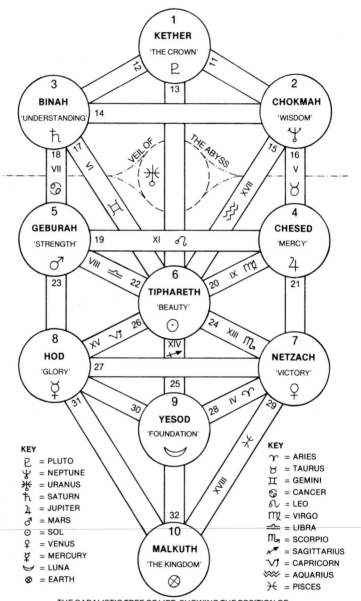

THE QABALISTIC TREE OF LIFE, SHOWING THE POSITION OF
THE SIGNS OF THE ZODIAC AND THEIR CORRESPONDING TAROT CARDS.

carried on the rising tide of confusion. The forces of opposition are far distant still; they present no immediate threat.

The Charioteer should calmly and with unhurried precision ensure that his chariot and steeds are prepared to contend with emergency. Such weaponry as he may be called upon to employ should also be gathered and made ready. It is an important time for the careful planning of action.

The forces of opposition are distant and conflict has yet to take place. The Charioteer therefore remains in a position of unexposed security. From his safe vantage point he can observe the movements of those in the distance and predict their intentions. There can be no surprise move made against him or his army.

To advance towards the horizon would not be fortuitous. It would precipitate unnecessary action. The Charioteer has been called only to make ready for battle; those in high command recognize that this is a time for the grouping of forces. Beyond the necessary activities of consolidation there is no indication that advance or retreat would prove of value.

Notes

The Charioteer of Tarot Trump VII descends from the powerful influence of Binah, therefore his mission is under the most accomplished guidance. The entrance of Sol seems to suggest the need for the regrouping of forces, a pause to take stock of the situation and adopt suitable safeguards. On the Tree of Life, Sol may be said to represent the mid-point of the Charioteer's destined course in the pursuit of his quest. He has descended from the heights; now is not the time to proceed further. Far better for the lower spheres to ascend to the higher, than the higher be consumed by the lower.

---

7 in 5

Correspondences
Netzach, 'Victory'; Venus. The Zodiacal Sign of Leo, the Lion; Tarot Trump XI 'Lust'.
Venus rules the element Fire; Leo is of Fire.

Main Principle   Venus in Atu XI 'Lust'.

The Title   Passionate union.

The Reading

The naked woman sits in rapture astride the mighty lion. Progress is made through the passionate union of strength and weakness.

The great wild lion permits himself to be ridden by the naked woman. The apparently weak and the manifestly strong have entered into unconventional union. We observe the brazen actions of those unconcerned with orthodox requirements and expectations.

Such actions are the mark of those destined to proceed beyond the limits achieved by the followers of convention.

When two opposite forces approach each other with passion and ardour, the concourse will produce one balanced force perfect in its equilibrium. Where equilibrium is established, all resistance is banished; progress is achieved without further opposition.

The Universe will no longer shield its glory but will freely yield up the Paths to attainment. The woman and lion conjoined will soar as a new star into the opening heavens.

Such is the reward for those who, being strong, embrace weakness, or being weak offer themselves up to the strong with passion, that they may through the agency of their love jointly seek their united perfection.

Notes

The fires of Leo and the fires of Venus are highly compatible. Together they merge into one steady flame of far-reaching brilliance. The main agent of this operation is love, represented by Venus, which serves to promote the woman and lion of Tarot Trump XI to a state of perfect balance and harmony. As the reading indicates, perfect balance is of the divine: it is an aspect of Unity wherein there is no conflict or dissent.

---

8 in 6

Correspondences

Hod, 'Glory'; Mercury. The Zodiacal Sign of Virgo, the Virgin; Tarot Trump IX 'The Hermit'.

Mercury rules the element Water; Virgo is of Earth.

Main Principle   Mercury in Atu IX 'The Hermit'.

The Title   Concern.

The Reading

Here we observe the small becoming expanded and adopting importance beyond its worth. This leads to concern, and time spent in worried deliberation.

When the small becomes expanded and brings concern, we see the weak striving to bring attention to itself. What should be content with its position and status rises up to claim a prominance which it cannot justify. The normal order of events then becomes disturbed. What should be calm and untroubled becomes worrisome. Attention must then be given to the seat of the disturbance; useful time is wasted in resolving the problem of arranging matters back into their rightful order.

When the small strives to become great, dissatisfaction is at the root of the impulse. Satisfaction does not cry out for change. When dissatisfaction seeks to bring change by making foolish or empty claims, only further unhappiness will materialise. The small itself will find grief its only reward after long and active labour, while those who are disturbed by the petty strivings of the small are distracted from their important duties. Thus the circle of discontent becomes expanded, and many are caught up in its distraction.

It is clear that the small should accept its position. By striving to make itself more agreeable and wise greatness will come without it being claimed falsely. True and lasting strength will then replace the foolish tendency to weakness. Those who are disturbed by the behaviour of the small need only to bide their time and pursue worthy goals, for the echoes of the false voice will not endure overlong.

Notes

The watery aspect of Mercury swamps the earthy Sign of Virgo, with the result that the Earth of Virgo becomes disturbed and displaced in a confusing swirl. This is a curious situation, particularly as Mercury reaches its Dignity in Virgo. But one of the side effects of Mercury in Virgo is a tendency to become overconcerned with matters of little importance, which necessarily detracts one from essentially important affairs. This explains the 'petty strivings of the small' referred to in the reading.

9 in 7

Correspondences
Yesod, 'Foundation'; Luna. The Zodiacal Sign of Libra, the Balances;
Tarot Trump VIII 'Adjustment'.
    Luna rules the element Air; Libra is of Air.

Main Principle   Luna in Atu VIII 'Adjustment'.

The Title   Ending of decrease.

The Reading

The Universe proceeds from chaos to order in regulated degrees. Having
reached a state of order the Universe must then return to chaos; thus the
cycles of change appear and depart. All things are allotted to their
season.

Here we observe the ending of decrease. The declining elements come
to rest in a state of confusion; original perfection is lost. In such
confusion chaos is born, but from chaos will spring the way to order.

The phases of increase and decline are governed by natural law, which
is applied regardless of the will of man.

Those who seek order, and the satisfaction that comes from stability,
observe the elements as they increase and understand that decline must
follow in its time. When decline comes and confusion arises, comfort is
obtained from the knowledge that ascent and progress follow. Without
change, ascent and progress could not take place.

By making provisions for the effects of decline advantage will be
gained. Resources will be protected, and the succeeding season of
increase met from a position of strength.

Notes

The airy nature of Luna serves to sway the balances of Libra; increase
and decrease then revolve about a common centre. On the Tree of Life
Luna represents the penultimate stage of the descent of Spirit into
matter; the return to Spirit or the ideal is but one step away. Events now
proceed to their lowest ebb as a consequence of inescapable factors. But
the return to the ideal will come when the present set of circumstances
have run their course.

3 in 8

Correspondences
Binah, 'Understanding'; Saturn. The Zodiacal Sign of Scorpio, the Scorpion; Tarot Trump XIII 'Death'.

Saturn rules the element Water; Scorpio is of Water.

Main Principle   Saturn in Atu XIII 'Death'.

The Title   Reducing to stillness.

The Reading

Beneficial change cannot take place when restriction is king. When all things are reduced to stillness, as when the very harvest itself does not grow, there can be no gathering in of useful fruits.

Here we observe motion reducing to stillness. The harvest does not grow; the harvester sits unmoving, waiting for the return of light and progress. The darkness of night predominates.

When the light of dawn brings warmth and reassurance, motion and progress will rise anew. Both harvest and harvester will then stir. But until that time no advantage will come in this forsaken Path where restriction is master of all.

Notes

Saturn entering the Path of Tarot Trump XIII produces a total cessation of all progress. It is the restricting activity of Saturn brought to the surface and exposed in its most cold and ruthless light. There seems little to be gained from an analysis of the interaction of the elements involved; the negative nature of the reading is clear enough and ought to deter anyone from proceeding under these circumstances. Note well that Tarot Trump XIII simply indicates a process of change; too superficial an interpretation must always be avoided.

4 in 9

Correspondences
Chesed, 'Mercy'; Jupiter. The Zodiacal Sign of Sagittarius, the Archer;
Tarot Trump XIV 'Art'.
  Jupiter rules the element Water; Sagittarius is of Fire.

Main Principle   Jupiter in Atu XIV 'Art'.

The Title   United Effort.

The Reading

Here we observe aspiration achieving its desire. The union of compatible
forces transforms a thing dull and inert into vital activity. This leads to
justifiable and happy optimism.

  Such transformation as is here indicated requires the willing
submission of contributing elements. The coming together of things in
helpful cooperation marks the beginning of profitable works. The
knowledge of forthcoming success generates optimism and enthusiasm
where once was despondency and disappointment.

  Action has been taken at the proper time and in a just manner; there
will now be encouraging growth and increasing stability.

  The union of compatible forces creates a united effort; all things work
together in the pursuit of common ambition. Such unification of
intention brings swift and unwavering progress; it is as the flight of an
arrow towards its mark.

  If ambition and excitement does not lead to the oversight of important
detail, happy optimism will continue to increase as desire is fulfilled.

Notes

The enormously powerful energies of Jupiter are positively and
benevolently aspected in the Path of Tarot Trump XIV. The Jupiterian
qualities of stability and expansion are precisely those required for the
successful completion of the alchemical process indicated by the trump.
Steady application turns the dross into gold. This in the world of
mundane affairs is indicative of considerable good fortune.

5 in 10

Correspondences
Geburah, 'Strength'; Mars. The Zodiacal Sign of Capricorn, the Goat;
Tarot Trump XV 'The Devil'.
    Mars rules the element Fire; Capricorn is of Earth.

Main Principle   Mars in Atu XV 'The Devil'.

The Title   Unrelenting steps.

The Reading
The Mountain Goat ascends the arduous slopes that he may reach the
high summit and there obtain his reward. How like the Mountain Goat is
the man who seeks great achievement; together they journey from the
lower to the higher, together they diligently ascend the slopes of
endeavour in the pursuit of exalted success.

When such a journey is undertaken with reluctance, as one who
proceeds under command, progress will be slow and little benefit is
gained. But when the slopes are approached with enthusiasm and
vitality the ground is quickly crossed, and the lowlands swiftly recede.

Here we observe the presence of enthusiasm and vitality upon the
mountain slopes. The high peak is held firmly in view; obstructions
looming to deflect the weak do not endure.

One who steps forth upon such a quest has previously surveyed the
measure of the heights and knows well the immensity of the task. A
mountain cannot be underestimated in its might. Therefore the enormity
of the journey is understood; there will be no unsuspected toil.

But when enthusiasm and vitality fuel the ascent the slopes will be
traversed with unrelenting steps. The peak will be attained without
undue delay; the obstructions that arise will be vanquished. Thus a great
work of endurance is accomplished without the weakening of inner
resolve.

Notes
The fiery nature of Mars (the god of war) is well aspected in the Sign of
Capricorn; indeed Mars is 'Exalted' therein. The natural quiescence of
earth is transformed into an active, even exhilarated state. Thus the
Mountain Goat (a reflection of Tarot Trump XV) is no longer a docile
creature but a force to be reckoned with. No matter how daunting the
task ahead may seem, energy and resolve will serve to bring about the
desired success.

6 in 11

Correspondences
Tiphareth, 'Beauty'; Sol. The Zodiacal Sign of Aquarius, the Water-bearer; Tarot Trump XVII 'The Star'.

Sol rules the element Air; Aquarius is of Air.

Main Principle   Sol in Atu XVII 'The Star'.

The Title   Establishment of reformation.

The Reading

Here we observe the rising up of great creativity. The Path now leads from the centre of attainment to the heights of glory. It is the setting out towards exalted success, and the beginning of marvellous works.

It is a time for the pushing back of restriction and the establishment of reformation. From this will flow the deeds that build up new lands.

The power of creativity is great; it builds up mountains and forms deep lakes; it breathes life into what was not living. Creativity has no equal; it is at the heart of everything in the Universe. It cannot be seen, nor touched. It is known only by the fruits of its labour, and by the passion that flows from its silent presence.

The great artist is the mate and channel of creativity. Together they unite and release the outpourings of their union as works of beauty. Even the lesser artist, the common man, touches upon the silent presence and establishes his works according to his will. Without creativity the great artist and the lesser man would not be; they would be void in the empty womb of the Infinite.

Therefore when creativity is seen to rise up with vigour enough to push back restriction, it is a sign of powerful and fortunate change. The establishment of reformation, the turning about of things to new order, will lead to deep and rewarding contentment.

Notes

Tarot Trump XVII occupies the 15th Path which leads from Tiphareth, Beauty, to Chokmah, Wisdom, the former being referred to Sol and the latter, across the dividing Abyss, to Neptune. The sphere of Sol is the heart of the Tree of Life and is of considerable importance when viewed as a seat of power. It is from this position that the Star now commences the final thrust towards the most exalted and illuminated reaches of attainment.

7 in 12

Correspondences
Netzach, 'Victory'; Venus. The Zodiacal Sign of Pisces, the Fishes; Tarot Trump XVIII 'The Moon'.

Venus rules the element Fire; Pisces is of Water.

Main Principle   Venus in Atu XVIII 'The Moon'.

The Title   Echoes of delight.

The Reading

There is cause for rejoicing when the dark and dangerous byways are successfully traversed by the intrepid seeker.

When malevolence and benighted places are overcome and beauty prevails, the Universe itself trembles in the echoes of delight.

Yet in such victory there lurks a subtle danger. Rejoicing in the pleasures of victory may lead to gross indulgence designed to serve no noble end. This will undo all that has been accomplished. Ill-fortune will then arise.

When the intrepid seeker has justifiable cause for rejoicing, let him observe the rules of Art that discipline may guide his flow of rapture. Through the constructive channelling of rapture, great and enduring works are created. In this manner even society benefits; the people will come from all quarters to share in the tangible product of joy.

Only wisdom, strength and determination can overcome the mighty powers of malevolent and benighted places; such admirable qualities ought not to be abandoned for the sake of ignoble pleasures.

Further progress is indicated if discipline is now conjoined with rapture. Foolish indulgence will swiftly reverse all success.

Notes

Here the fiery nature of Venus brings beneficial light and warmth to the darkling waters of Pisces. Tarot Trump XVIII very clearly illustrates these darkling waters; indeed the whole message of the card is one of ill-omen. But the entrance of Venus serves to check these negative qualities.

On the Tree of Life Tarot Trump XVIII actually leads to the sphere of Venus; this explains why the reading suggests a goal accomplished. The danger of falling prey to the vice of the sphere, which is lust, or dissipation, is also cautioned against.

8 in 1

Correspondences
Hod, 'Glory'; Mercury. The Zodiacal Sign of Aries, the Ram; Tarot
Trump IV 'The Emperor'.
   Mercury rules the element Water; Aries is of Fire.

Main Principle   Mercury in Atu IV 'The Emperor'.

The Title   Unthinking haste.

The Reading

When the young Emperor is newly risen to the throne, the seers of the
Empire will scrutinize his judgements, that they may foretell the future
of the reign.

   If the new Emperor has no experience of leadership, allowances will be
made for early misjudgements. In such a case the future of the reign
cannot be foretold with great accuracy or ease.

   But when the newly enthroned young Emperor is experienced in
command, his first words sound the future of the reign and of the Empire
itself.

   Here we observe the newly enthroned young Emperor who has
achieved prominence by the might of his will; thus he has experience of
command. When such a one is now seen to act too swiftly, even
foolishly, in important matters of state, the peoples of the Empire need
not consult the seers to determine the future.

   How should the advisors approach this Emperor; what counsel should
they proffer to one who rises to greatness only to cloud his reign with
unthinking haste?

   If the Emperor is wise he will realise his error by the nature of its
results. Thus he will not reject the good counsel of his advisors and they
need not fear to approach him.

   In the quiet of his chamber the Emperor should meditate upon the
origin and outcome of his rashness, and learn the value of wise
deliberation in every matter of state.

Notes

Mercury is the winged messenger of the gods and is traditionally
recognised as the fount of sudden, inspirational knowledge. But in the
domain of the Emperor the effect tends to be one of undisciplined fantasy
rather than sound, upsurging wisdom. This is because Aries is Cardinal
and Fire, and so tends to instability. There is not the developed strength
to bring Mercury to heel. The need for caution is indicated.

9 in 2

Correspondences
Yesod, 'Foundation'; Luna. The Zodiacal Sign of Taurus, the Bull; Tarot Trump V 'The Hierophant'.

Luna rules the element Air; Taurus is of Earth.

Main Principle   Luna in Atu V 'The Hierophant'.

The Title   Advantageous increase.

The Reading

The Hierophant reaches his elevated status by following the dictates of his true will and observing the propriety of his deeds. Attention to the calling of his inner voice opens many doors; he stands in a position of authority and is attended by disciples.

The Hierophant who ceases to harken to his inner voice and abandons his Path for the sake of another will fall from his high position, and his disciples will foresake him. But the Hierophant who returns constantly to the gates of vision will gather virtue and learning. By adhering to his chosen way he will be raised up in the halls of knowledge. His disciples will benefit.

Here we observe the Hierophant who is truly inspired, for he has unlocked the door to the treasure house of visions. From this springs knowledge of all the Paths leading to the light and the dark. The Hierophant will know the true values of all things and the benefits of pursuing praiseworthy goals.

One who has entered the seat of knowledge and knows the true value of all things will choose a Path of worthy progress. Thus there will be a continued advance. The Hierophant's disciples will benefit from his wisdom; they will follow in the light of his example and rise to new status.

All things therefore enter a phase of new and advantageous increase.

Notes

Luna in the Path of Tarot Trump V has the effect of heightening the perceptions of the Hierophant, with the result that he is able to pursue his tasks with greater vision and subsequent success. In a sense the Hierophant has been 'wed'; he has met his complementary aspect and the union has brought forth a child greater than its parents. This is the subject and object of all true magick.

3 in 3

Correspondences
Binah, 'Understanding'; Saturn. The Zodiacal Sign of Gemini, the Twins; Tarot Trump VI 'The Lovers'.
   Saturn rules the element Water; Gemini is of Air.

Main Principle   Saturn in Atu VI 'The Lovers'.

The Title   Firm foundations.

The Reading

The Lovers have chosen well their Path. The coming together of two separate elements into a state of Unity was their objective; the chosen way now leads inexorably towards that goal.

   There will be no sudden thunder-flashes of violent change, no fierce whirlwinds to mark the turning about of things long established. Rather there will be the placid arrangement of the elements into their destined order. Tranquility will mark the attainment of this high success.

   The union of two elements in such a placid and tranquil manner presages the establishment of order that is destined to endure through the years. Hastily built is hastily fallen; stability is the child of serenity.

   Now is a time for the careful ordering of affairs, and the measurement of resources. The assessment of all things of value will assist in the laying down of firm foundations.

   Turbulence, division and uncertainty are shadows now consigned to a darker past. Ahead there shines the steady light of great attainment and reward. The pinnacle of success approaches.

Notes

Saturn is a much misaligned sphere, often denounced as the bringer of destruction through slow decay, or the harbinger of things malefic. But Saturn does have a very positive aspect, and in Gemini this aspect is to the fore. Saturn occupies the Sephirah Binah on the Tree of Life, to which elevation Tarot Trump VI aspires. The appearance of Saturn would therefore seem to indicate aspirations fulfilled; the Lovers are seen to have crossed the dark Abyss which separates Saturn from the lower spheres.

4 in 4

Correspondences
Chesed, 'Mercy'; Jupiter. The Zodiacal Sign of Cancer, the Crab; Tarot Trump VII 'The Chariot'.

Jupiter rules the element Water; Cancer is of Water.

Main Principle   Jupiter in Atu VII 'The Chariot'.

The Title   Contentment comes.

The Reading

The Charioteer does not linger in his own familiar land. It is his destined way to proceed swiftly onward, until the will of his superiors is fulfilled. He so continues on his allotted Path, but his is not a search for strife nor a journey of conquering for the purpose of gain.

The Charioteer proceeds as a seeker. He seeks the establishment of peace and unity through the dissemination of the message he bears from those in high authority, which is a message of hope, a deliverance of divine law.

Here we observe the Charioteer meeting with success. He enters a land of stability, wherein peace and unity are the aspiration of all.

His message falls on kindly and receptive ears. He is welcomed into the great palace itself, and is there received as a brother.

Having found a land in sympathy with the great and noble vision of his superiors, the Charioteer will be exalted and encouraged. His success will fortify and enhance his future progress. It is a time of reward for labour spent, and for the recognition of loyal services. Contentment comes on golden wings.

When the Charioteer continues further on his journey his present success will sustain him during times of temporary failure or dismay.

Notes

The powerful stabilising effect of Jupiter serves well the unstabilised Sign of Cancer. It is the great torrent of a waterfall brought to the placid calm of a lake. The Charioteer of Tarot Trump VII ceases for a while his eternal quest; he meets a virtual reflection of his own compulsions. The result is satisfaction.

No state of Being can exist forever, and the time must come when the Charioteer reins up his steeds once more. But he will set out from a much higher level of achievement.

5 in 5

Correspondences
Geburah, 'Strength'; Mars. The Zodiacal Sign of Leo, the Lion; Tarot Trump XI 'Lust'.

Mars rules the element Fire; Leo is of Fire.

Main Principle   Mars in Atu XI 'Lust'.

The Title   Turmoil opposes progress.

The Reading

If the naked woman is to journey astride the mighty lion, understanding and trust are qualities necessary both above and below if the destination is to be reached without grief.

The woman has shed all that she has in pursuit of her lion; the lion has duly accepted her presence. The journey has begun; the naked woman is upon the kingly beast. The sacrifices of pursuit have been recognized and an alliance forged between weak and strong.

In such an alliance strength and weakness merge together in one united force. There is harmony born of understanding and trust.

When one united force advances with great determination it can only deteriorate in the presence of overwhelming opposition. But even this deterioration need not result in total decay if the bond of harmony prevails. Where understanding and trust continue to operate without deviation, harmony itself will not be destroyed. Where harmony exists, the Path to attainment remains ever open.

Here we observe the presence of great turmoil. Such turmoil opposes progress. The understanding and trust between woman and lion should not be allowed to falter.

If the alliance between weak and strong is broken, all progress will cease. The opportunity to advance will have been lost needlessly.

The turmoil we observe marks the birth-pangs of change; the harnessing of inflamed passion will lead to desirable success. By proceeding as one united force the woman and the lion will stand in triumph at the ending of their Path; the turmoil of change should not stay them from their destiny.

Notes

Tarot Trump XI spans the Path on the Tree of Life between the spheres of Mars and Jupiter. Without the balancing presence of Jupiter the aggressive nature of Mars rapidly seeks control. The indication is that a partnership of some form becomes threatened; the elements held in balance find their equilibrium disturbed. But this condition does not appear to present a major obstacle to success; rather it suggests initial difficulty prior to the objective being won.

---

6 in 6

Correspondences
Tiphareth, 'Beauty'; Sol. The Zodiacal Sign of Virgo, the Virgin; Tarot Trump IX 'The Hermit'.
  Sol rules the element Air; Virgo is of Earth.

Main Principle   Sol in Atu IX 'The Hermit'.

The Title   No movement.

The Reading

Here we observe the Hermit building up his hermitage. There will be progress but no movement.

  Building up what is useful and to hand brings good fortune; turning existing resources to advantage ensures that maximum benefits are obtained from them. Until this is achieved there is little to be gained from seeking out new horizons.

  The premature departure from things of value undermines past attempts to create enduring satisfaction. Acquaintances will cease to offer their assistance to one who is seen to be wasteful of resources. This will lead to enmity and regret.

  By building up his hermitage the Hermit will create a worthy and useful centre for his labours. Attending to that which is closest to his immediate needs brings the reward of contentment born of sufficiency. Unlooked-for help and encouragement will arrive; assistance is given willingly by those who admire good husbandry.

  Thus progress will be made without unnecessary movement. Stability and satisfaction follow the building up of what is useful and to hand. The Hermit enters the hermitage and receives enlightenment; knowledge comes of the way to proceed in accord with what is right.

47

Notes

Tarot Trump IX occupies the 20th Path on the Tree of Life between the Sephiroth Tiphareth and Chesed. The present dominance of Sol in the Path of the trump would therefore suggest the process of organization made prior to undertaking any new venture in the future. The underlying inference throughout the reading is that prudence must be exercised, but upward progress is still possible.

---

7 in 7

Correspondences
Netzach, 'Victory'; Venus. The Zodiacal Sign of Libra, the Balances; Tarot Trump VIII 'Adjustment'.
  Venus rules the element Fire; Libra is of Air.

Main Principle   Venus in Atu VIII 'Adjustment'.

The Title   Gratifying harmony.

The Reading

A great artist assembles his work from elements that combine in pleasing harmony. The building up of his composition is a labour that gives living expression to what he feels is beautiful and balanced. Nothing will be incompatible; all will blend together in an order regulated yet relaxed. The finished composition will represent the ideal as envisaged by him; reality will be conveyed according to his conception of what he sees. His completed labour will satisfy himself and give pleasure to others.

  Here we observe the structuring of events and resources to build towards a desired objective. This is carried out in the manner of a great artist, for all things are combined in gratifying harmony.

  All things here come together in their rightful order and with pleasing compatibility. The result is continuous satisfaction. The objective is envisaged and the image brings pleasure; the coming together of events in a harmonious manner serves to illustrate the virtue of the objective, and the propriety of all undertakings in pursuit of the quest.

  As the great artist surveys his completed labour and experiences pleasure, so here shall the seeker gain pleasure both from the pursuit of the quest, in which events and resources blend together in an order regulated yet relaxed, and from the achievement of the objective itself, in which the ideal as conceived will be realized. The completed labour will afford great satisfaction to those involved.

Notes

The fiery nature of Venus is well aspected in the airy Sign of Libra. Fire disintegrates and transmutes the gross into the fine; air encourages the presence of fire. The requirement of Tarot Trump VIII is for just such a harmonious combination of elements in the fight against disorder. The transmutation of unstable elements is made possible; progress towards perfection continues.

---

8 in 8

Correspondences
Hod, 'Glory'; Mercury. The Zodiacal Sign of Scorpio, the Scorpion; Tarot Trump XIII 'Death'.
  Mercury rules the element Water; Scorpio is of Water.

Main Principle   Mercury in Atu XIII 'Death'.

The Title   According to desire.

The Reading

The Universe is changing constantly; throughout the Infinite there is advance and retreat, growth and decay. As with the greater Universe above so it is with the smaller Universe below in the affairs of man.
  Knowledge of the processes leading to growth and decay will advance one on the quest for success. Without such knowledge one is at the mercy of the capricious fates; change for good or ill takes place regardless of one's desire.
  One who possesses the appropriate knowledge is able to place himself in a fortunate position at an auspicious moment. Success is then achieved where others of lesser ability fail.
  Here we observe one who has suitable knowledge of the ways of growth and decay. He is as the Reaper who, knowing the order of the

seasons, strides forth with his scythe at the approach of harvest time. Progress is achieved by one who knows when to advance in accord with the seasons.

When advantage is taken of worthy opportunity the activities of the capricious fates will be diminished. As the Reaper cuts down that which is ripe, so will the wise seeker of success gather in what is helpful and cast out what is not. In this way good things are made to prosper.

Change now occurs according to desire. The pursuit of success will meet with good fortune.

Notes

Tarot Trump XIII indicates a process of change. Into the realm of this trump there now appears the inspirational force of Mercury, and the powers of applied thought. The inference is that circumstances are about to alter as a result of studiously considered action. The form of change generally represented by Tarot Trump XIII is that of the modification of existing conditions, rather than the creation of something entirely new and unrelated.

---

9 in 9

Correspondences
Yesod, 'Foundation'; Luna. The Zodiacal Sign of Sagittarius, the Archer; Tarot Trump XIV 'Art'.
   Luna rules the element Air; Sagittarius is of Fire.

Main Principle   Luna in Atu XIV 'Art'.

The Title   Fulfilment of aspiration.

The Reading

As an arrow leaves the bow and wings its way freely towards its mark, so here do we observe the unhindered passage of aspiration soaring to reach its fulfilment.

The restrictions of demands from society and acquiantances are here removed through the severance of unworthy ties. The falling away of encumbrances permits the freedom to advance in accord with will; this will bring great satisfaction and constructive progress.

New horizons approach and are explored; opportunity arises for the exploration of rewarding pursuits. The time for change comes and is embraced; stillness yields to beneficial motion.

The intelligent use of change brings the fulfilment of aspiration, but carelessness will lead to grief. Too eager an approach will encourage the entry of error and oversight; forethought and attention to the feelings of those from whom assistance is sought will maintain untroubled progress.

The tides of fortune ebb and flow; the seizing of an advantageous current adds happiness to the pursuit of aspiration's worthy goal.

Notes

Tarot Trump XIV mediates between the Sephirah Tiphareth and the lower aspected Sephirah Yesod. From another point of view it represents the seeker ascending from the lower realms of aspiration and capricious change to the higher spheres of the fixed and eternal. This view is given substance by the symbol of the Sagittarian arrow which is directed upward, indicating the potential of ascent to the highest after the initial descent or 'fall'. The reading suggests that this journey of ascent is now about to take place, with fortunate consequences.

---

3 in 10

Correspondences
Binah, 'Understanding'; Saturn. The Zodiacal Sign of Capricorn, the Goat; Tarot Trump XV 'The Devil'.
Saturn rules the element Water; Capricorn is of Earth.

Main Principle   Saturn in Atu XV 'The Devil'.

The Title   Exalted success.

The Reading

The seeker moves from the land to the heavens in search of attainment, as the Mountain Goat ascends the arduous slopes to win the lofty peak. Obstruction, danger and diversion present themselves; hungry chasms must be traversed. The achievement of great success is not accomplished without diligence and devotion. Neither is progress on the Path to attainment possible if knowledge of the way to the goal itself is absent. Without such knowledge the seeker wanders without filling the hidden yet insistent hunger of the soul. But when the way to the goal is known, and assiduously pursued, the achievement of the lofty peak is made possible, even within one lifetime.

Here we observe one who advances upon the slopes of aspiration with diligence and devotion. Suitable resources have been employed to good effect; the building up of a stable base has supplied a broad and strong foundation for the reaches of higher effort. Thus the seeker has created from his life a mountain of wisdom; it ascends to the heights with resolute and immovable firmness. Therefore there will be exalted success.

Destiny has long revealed its secret; the seeker proceeds with measured steps to claim what is his. Danger and obstacles are encountered and vanquished with masterly ease. Diligence permits of no downfall; devotion brings lasting reward.

Notes

When Saturn enters the Path of Tarot Trump XV the figure represented by the card arrives face to face with his higher Self and is therefore fully equipped to sieze his revealed destiny and wring from it every possible advantage. The Devil, or Satan, is merely an aspect of one's own unconscious which in the uninitiated will always remain a separate, dark and seemingly independent entity. In a purely astrological sense Saturn is said to rule the Sign of Capricorn, which reaffirms the link between the planet and the trump.

4 in 11

Correspondences

Chesed, 'Mercy'; Jupiter. The Zodiacal Sign of Aquarius, the Water-bearer; Tarot Trump XVII 'The Star'.

Jupiter rules the element Water; Aquarius is of Air.

Main Principle   Jupiter in Atu XVII 'The Star'.

The Title   Happiness accompanies abundance.

The Reading

Water flows from the mountain springs and fills the empty lakes below. Laughter echoes from the high peak; those dwelling by the lakes throw open their windows that good fortune may enter. Children play in lush pastures and make crowns from scented flowers.

The filling of empty lakes awakens dormant life; new growth appears and gives welcome comfort to those in need. Thus is established the anticipated season of increase.

Laughter in the high peaks signals the joy of the gods. By opening windows to such joy, good fortune is encouraged to enter; the opening of closed places at the proper time enhances the ingress of opportunity. Progress is achieved when opportunity is welcomed and turned to advantage.

Children play happily when care and want are absent. Lush pastures abound when all the elements are exalted. When crowns are fashioned from scented flowers in place of common weeds, economy of means is no longer a consideration of importance. Happiness accompanies abundance.

When the times of austerity are done, the people of the land are free to engage themselves in useful social activity. There is a coming together of the people in contentment and friendship. It is a time of great harmony and pleasure.

The opening of closed places to opportunity reaps great benefit when society gathers to celebrate good fortune.

Notes

The regal nature of Jupiter meets the light of creativity issuing from The Star. The world is duly transformed. Tarot Trump XVII is also referred to the Hebrew letter Hé, which means window. The idea of a window or portal opening up to permit the entrance of good fortune is explicit in the reading, and should be interpreted as an encouragement to pursue any worthwhile opportunity which has presented itself. As a further point of interest Jupiter is sometimes referred to as the All Father, whereas The Star is a glyph of the Supreme Goddess.

5 in 12

Correspondences
Geburah, 'Strength'; Mars. The Zodiacal Sign of Pisces, the Fishes;
Tarot Trump XVIII 'The Moon'.
  Mars rules the element Fire; Pisces is of Water.

Main Principle   Mars in Atu XVIII 'The Moon'.

The Title   Along dark byways.

The Reading

The weakling enters the realm of shadows and falls prey to fear and
catastrophe; the strong-willed enters and emerges victorious. Progress is
achieved when elements are positioned in places that will not overwhelm
them.
  Here we observe great activity advancing along dark byways. There is
great strength and determination behind the activity, therefore the
adversaries that lurk in the shadows restrain themselves from making an
attack, and content themselves with their malicious preparations.
  Yet even though adversaries are subdued, the darkness of the byway
remains. Such light as appears is brief and confounding; relief comes but
is gone in the instant. Raised hopes are dashed in the return of darkness.
  In such a place one cannot place faith in the way ahead. The
appropriate strategy is to allow for all contingencies; in this alone lies the
secret of future progress.
  The qualities of activity, strength and determination are valuable
allies when the way is unclear. By employing such allies in the pursuit of
what is right, success will be snatched from the teeth of darkness and the
traveller will emerge victorious.

Notes

The treacherous Path of darkness as illustrated by Tarot Trump XVIII is
successfully traversed by discipline and courage. These are qualities
exhibited by Mars in plenty, for Mars is the god of war. Progress will be
made through action executed with all the vigour of a military
campaign. As ever where Mars is concerned, care is required in that a
lack of sufficient discipline will result in too much force being applied to
the matter in hand, leading to subsequent recrimination.

6 in 1

Correspondences
Tiphareth, 'Beauty'; Sol. The Zodiacal Sign of Aries, the Ram; Tarot
Trump IV 'The Emperor'.
    Sol rules the element Air; Aries is of Fire.

Main Principle   Sol in Atu IV 'The Emperor'.

The Title   Certainty.

The Reading

An Empire is a reflection of the will of its Emperor. The word and deed
issuing from the throne builds up or casts down the very realm itself.

When the Emperor is weak or unlearned, darkness falls upon the
Empire and growth is stagnated. But when the Emperor is capable and
wise, growth and progress are achieved.

Here we observe the Emperor standing at the threshold of new and
important developments. Through his careful labours he reaches a
zenith of his reign. Diligence and firmness of will now yield their reward;
growth and progress come.

From hope and aspiration he passes into certainty. Such is his ability
to obtain advantage from minor opportunity as well as great, that he
will be applauded as a worthy leader of men.

When expectations become certainty through the success of careful
labours, tribute is paid to those who so succeed.

But success should not tempt the Emperor to abandon all caution. He
must still proceed with the precise judgement proper to his status. With
diligence and firmness of will the Emperor will create a new and
enduring Empire upon the foundations of the old.

Notes

Here we see the benevolent energies of Sol at their best, bringing stability
and unification to the inherently unstable Emperor. The fluctuating
nature of Cardinal Aries is calmed and smoothed by Sol's entrance; the
result is wholly satisfactory. This is due to the position of Sol on the Tree
of Life. Being situated between Kether and Malkuth its principle
function is to balance and coordinate. A major achievement of this
process is the bringing to light of one's true will, which once discovered
cannot be baulked of fulfilment.

7 in 2

Correspondences
Netzach, 'Victory'; Venus. The Zodiacal Sign of Taurus, the Bull; Tarot Trump V 'The Hierophant'.
Venus rules the element Fire; Taurus is of Earth.

Main Principle   Venus in Atu V 'The Hierophant'.

The Title   Peaceful advantage.

The Reading

The winning of honourable favour and assistance in society is not accomplished by one of brutal or selfish disposition, but by one who reflects the ideals of those whom he approaches or with whom he resides.

When worthy benefits come to one who seeks them we see happiness and satisfaction both in the seeker and in the providing society itself. This furthers harmony, and leads to the mutual exchange of labour's good fortune.

Here we observe one who seeks favour and assistance, and is granted generously that which he desires. Therefore we see society and the individual in harmony; this indicates the general arrangement of elements in useful organization. From this stems progress and achievement in many worthy directions. Wealth comes and brings peaceful advantage.

When desire is fulfilled we see satisfaction and pleasure in both giver and receiver alike. The giver retires to replenish his resources that further satisfaction and pleasure may be given and shared; the receiver retires to employ his good fortune to useful effect.

By reflecting the ideals of those whom one approaches, favour is won and benefits sought are obtained. The intelligent and honourable use of assistance brings later acclaim, and leads to the opening up of further opportunity.

Notes

Although the sphere of Venus is situated far below the realm of Tarot Trump V, the appearance of this planet in the trump's Path indicates a beneficial increase in self-expression and pleasure. The fire of Venus does not burn the earth of Taurus but provides the right degree of warmth and light necessary for fertile growth. Traditionally, Venus is said to rule the Sign of Taurus.

8 in 3

Correspondences
Hod, 'Glory'; Mercury. The Zodiacal Sign of Gemini, the Twins; Tarot
Trump VI 'The Lovers'.
 Mercury rules the element Water, Gemini is of Air.

Main Principle   Mercury in Atu VI 'The Lovers'.

The Title   Necessary duty.

The Reading

The Lovers desire to unite and become as one. If there is disagreement
between them harmony will decline and the achievement of their union
will be delayed. But when the Lovers act in perfect accord the
achievement of an objective is swiftly advanced.

Here we observe the Lovers progressing on the Path to their union.
The elements are in their rightful places; all things work together in
agreeable cooperation. Yet the Path itself is now filled with
dispassionate calculation. The Lovers do not proceed with the passion
and ardour of mutual devotion, therefore we observe them in the
execution of a necessary duty.

Dispassionate calculation will bring great success. Progress is assured
when duty is executed without delay or regret. Such deeds as are
necessary to maintain harmony or achievement are now swiftly and
precisely accomplished. Concerted effort towards a common goal brings
joint and beneficial reward.

The unhesitating fulfilment of duty indicates strength of will and
purpose. When this is displayed by two acting in perfect accord, notable
success is made possible. Those who witness such success present their
acclaim; friendships develop and prosper, horizons are increased.
Growth and good fortune are then established in all quarters.

Notes

Mercury is the bringer of divine counsel. It is therefore appropriate that
he rules the Sign of Gemini, where the Lovers of Tarot Trump VI require
guidance on the Path that will lead them to the God-Head of Unity.
Allowed a free hand, Mercury will certainly bring success of a kind, but
it is likely to be devoid of all concern for emotion. It is the work and
success of the scientist rather than the artist.

9 in 4

Correspondences
Yesod, 'Foundation'; Luna. The Zodiacal Sign of Cancer, the Crab; Tarot Trump VII 'The Chariot'.

Luna rules the element Air; Cancer is of Water.

Main Principle   Luna in Atu VII 'The Chariot'.

The Title   Working together.

The Reading

The Charioteer who must travel from the known to the unknown, as one who must travel through life itself, should know well the direction to be taken if the journey is to meet with success.

Failure upon such a journey is the mark of one who moves blindly, or without fortitude.

Here we observe the Charioteer embarking on a journey into the unknown. The territory before him is uncharted and alien.

The beginning of any journey is in itself a safe and untroubled act, for the traveller is surrounded by the known and familiar. But when the known and familiar have long receded, fortitude is necessary if progress is to continue. If fortitude is not matched with insight, blindness and misfortune will prevail when the darkness deepens.

Here the Charioteer is possessed of an instinct akin to that of a hunter. This he employs to utmost effect. Though the terrain ahead be in shadow or tortuous, the Charioteer will steer his craft with deft precision. He will anticipate obstacles and danger, and by anticipation avoid them.

The steeds that draw the chariot are sturdy and fleet of foot; the chariot is of the finest craftsmanship. All the elements are therefore working together in perfect harmony. The Charioteer is in a position conducive to good fortune; success now comes.

The uncharted terrain will be crossed without hazard, the journey accomplished swiftly.

Notes

The Cardinal Sign of Cancer is easily influenced by the entrance of Luna; it is the surging of the waters into waves in response to gale force winds. As the waves soar to their crested peaks, so does the Charioteer of Tarot Trump VII rise up to meet his challenge.

Luna represents the unconscious. It is this powerful resource which serves to guide the Charioteer on his intended journey through life. Without the benefits of intuition or survival instincts any traveller is in peril when in unfamiliar circumstances.

---

3 in 5

Correspondences
Binah, 'Understanding'; Saturn. The Zodiacal Sign of Leo, the Lion; Tarot Trump XI 'Lust'.
   Saturn rules the element Water; Leo is of Fire.

Main Principle   Saturn in Atu XI 'Lust'.

The Title   Beyond reach.

The Reading

The naked woman cast off all that she had in pursuit of her ambition; the lion took the naked woman upon his back. Together they ventured forth to overcome by unusual means the obstacles to success.

   The apparently weak and the manifestly strong have united in a common purpose; to achieve success in their quest, each according to their desire. The union of two opposites, such as woman and lion, joined together for the sake of mutual progress, brings dedicated collaboration to bear on all things. The natural resistance of opposition is transformed into a one-pointed will to succeed. Though obstacles are overcome easily by the might of such a will, success must depend on the goal being within reach. If the goal is too far distant, or set about with many wearying obstacles, initial impetus and vigour must inevitably decline.

   The sands of time flow unceasing; even the Universe must yield to the insistence of decay and the fatigue of endeavour.

   Here we observe the naked woman and the lion who can proceed no farther. Impetus and vigour are overcome by distance and restriction. The objective was beyond reach; the quest must fail.

   The woman and the lion must now withdraw. By remaining in each other's company they may yet find alternative routes to achieve future progress. A time will come when the conditions are more favourably inclined.

Notes

The noble fires of Leo do not respond well to the dark waters of Saturn. The natural dominance of Leo is severely weakened by the intrusion. The elements of Tarot Trump XI demand a measure of freedom and mobility if they are to progress; the appearance of Saturn in their Path has the effect of restricting their actions. Advance becomes impossibly difficult. Traditionally Saturn is said to be detrimentally aspected in Leo.

---

4 in 6

Correspondences
Chesed, 'Mercy'; Jupiter. The Zodiacal Sign of Virgo, the Virgin; Tarot Trump IX 'The Hermit'.
  Jupiter rules the element Water; Virgo is of Earth.

Main Principle   Jupiter in Atu IX 'The Hermit'.

The Title   True authority.

The Reading

Here we observe one who has drunk deep of the fount of knowledge within the hermitage. Useful lessons have been learned in life; the cause and effect of past achievements and failures have been recognised.

  Such knowledge permits the entry into new undertakings with increased and justified confidence. Capabilities will be revealed and exploited to full advantage.

  Thus the hermitage has served its purpose. Withdrawal from confusion, and a reassessment of the needs of Self, has brought forth stability and a clear vision of what must now be accomplished. A correctly formulated will to succeed will now lead to exalted success.

  One who has gained so much from the hermitage of life need not fear the consequences of his deeds. Having mastered so much of what is necessary to achieve progress he may advance with confidence in the propriety of his intentions and endeavours. He will advance with true authority, and command widespread respect.

He is as the prince who, having spent his time in scholarship and preparation, now ascends to the throne itself to take the place of his father.

Notes

Tarot Trump IX occupies the 20th Path on the Tree of Life between the Sephiroth Tiphareth and Chesed, Chesed being the objective to which the figure in the trump aspires. Thus we see the hermitage fulfilled in its purpose and the Hermit equipped to establish himself in the regal sphere of Jupiter. It is labour, devotion, will and diligence reaping its reward.

---

5 in 7

Correspondences
Geburah, 'Strength'; Mars. The Zodiacal Sign of Libra, the Balances; Tarot Trump VIII 'Adjustment'.
  Mars rules the element Fire, Libra is of Air.

Main Principle   Mars in Atu VIII 'Adjustment'.

The Title   Dispersed and estranged.

The Reading

Here we observe balance disturbed. Agreement on any issue is no longer achievable; what is right and proper is put beyond reach. Therefore we observe also the beginnings of discord and injustice.

  Division comes when balance is disturbed. The breaking up of established order follows. This will bring long standing, even permanent separation and contention. What might once have been a working unity becomes dispersed and estranged; concerted effort becomes dissent.

  The destruction of balance will achieve no virtuous ambition. Separation and contention marks a return to chaos, wherein nothing is accomplished and nothing endures save chaos itself. When this is accompanied by injustice, society will seek fair retribution. The return to a state of balance is then not achieved without much rebuilding of trust.

The wise man seeks to proceed without incurring unnecessary resistance and strife. By replacing what is taken out, peace and balance are maintained; this permits the untroubled development of ambition.

Notes

The fiery and turbulent nature of Mars conflicts with the still air of Libra. The placid environment of balance is destroyed. The case is not helped even by the location of Tarot Trump VIII on the Tree of Life; it actually connects with the Sephirah Geburah. This is because the mediating influence of Tiphareth, with which the trump also connects, is absent. Thus the aggressive martial qualities hold sway in the absence of the Solar forces of synthesis. The result is imbalance, and a breakdown of order follows.

---

6 in 8

Correspondences
Tiphareth, 'Beauty'; Sol. The Zodiacal Sign of Scorpio, the Scorpion; Tarot Trump XIII 'Death'.
   Sol rules the element Air; Scorpio is of Water.

Main Principle   Sol in Atu XIII 'Death'.

The Title   Time of respite.

The Reading

Here we observe the Reaper who wields his scythe with firmness and precision. He does not recoil from the duties laid before him. His devotion and dedication will have its reward; he enters a phase of great accomplishment.

   The Path of the Reaper is both difficult and demanding. He must cut down the surrounding growth of useless obstruction that he may achieve his desired harvest. This is the task of one who sets foot on the Path to attainment; the removal of encumbrances that success may be achieved.

   The scythe must fall even on cherished possessions as one advances, for in the advancing old beliefs and customs give way to new. This is the way of all worthy progress.

When encumbrances are cut away harmony prevails; there are no obstructions to satisfaction. During periods of harmony the Reaper's scythe is no longer required. Where harmony exists the action of cutting away is both unnecessary and futile. Therefore, a time of respite follows the fulfilment of harsh duties.

Exemplary actions will yield their nourishing fruit; recognition will be obtained for honest labour.

Notes

Tarot Trump XIII occupies the Path on the Tree of Life between Tiphareth, Beauty, and Netzach, Victory. Therefore the figure represented by the trump has here achieved the position to which he originally aspired, as it is now Tiphareth-Sol which is the predominant sphere of effect. The scythe is now about to become redundant, and the Reaper will proceed under another form on his way to Kether, the Crown.

---

7 in 9

Correspondences
Netzach, 'Victory'; Venus. The Zodiacal Sign of Sagittarius, the Archer; Tarot Trump XIV 'Art'.

Venus rules the element Fire; Sagittarius is of Fire.

Main Principle   Venus in Atu XIV 'Art'.

The Title   Dispersal.

The Reading

The Sun appears to circle the heavens, the Moon circles the spinning Earth. Throughout the Universe one observes the action of forces moving in balanced opposition. It is the manner by which the Universe seeks to avoid chaos and maintain harmony.

As in the Universe above so it is in the world of man. The proper arrangement of the elements of one's Being leads ultimately to peace and wisdom; the proper arrangement of social matters leads to success in the affairs of the world. The pursuit of rightful conduct brings the harmony and stability of balance into all things.

Indulgence in matters which are not designed to encourage stability will lead to the decline of harmony and the drawing apart of things once held in balanced opposition.

Here we observe the rising up of indulgence into the realm of balanced affairs. This will lead to the dispersal of useful organization.

Organization is acquired through the careful assembly of elements into constructive collaboration. Such labours require the following of precise plans. When indulgence arises to break down the achievements of building up we see ignorance triumphing over wisdom. Attraction towards worthless pursuits brings cause for great sorrow and regret.

The wise man observes the manner in which the Universe seeks to avoid chaos through the employment of balanced action, and endeavours to order his life accordingly.

Notes

The appearance of Venus in the Path of Tarot Trump XIV indicates circumstances which do not encourage the commitment necessary for genuine progress. One seems to become immersed in various pursuits without actually making any real progress in any of them. The figure represented by the trump has been overwhelmed by the vices of Venus, and decline follows accordingly.

---

8 in 10

Correspondences
Hod, 'Glory'; Mercury. The Zodiacal Sign of Capricorn, the Goat; Tarot Trump XV 'The Devil'.

Mercury rules the element Water; Capricorn is of Earth.

Main Principle   Mercury in Atu XV 'The Devil'.

The Title   Exploited.

The Reading

Sound and propitious beginnings, such as those that mark the foundation of eminence, or that give rise to enduring and admirable works, may originate in the casual and brief encounter of observer and opportunity, or in the dreamings of intelligence in idle repose. But the journey from beginning to eminence, or to enduring and admirable works, is not completed without much deliberate care and sagacity.

Here we observe the elements of sound and propitious beginnings under the skilful direction of one who will exact from them good fortune and progress. A deep knowledge of what is achievable is conjoined with a will to reach the heights of attainment.

This will lead to the profitable employment of every resource; even the small and inferior will be exploited to yield up their hidden and unexpected bounty. It is as the conduct of the cunning mountain goat who roams the slopes from the lower to the higher, and who finds sustenance even in barren places as he draws nigh the sunlit peak.

The deep knowledge of what is achievable will bring success; deliberate care and sagacity will assist the acquisition of objectives, and forbear the presence of regret born of failure.

Notes

Tarot Trump XV occupies the Path leading from Hod to Tiphareth, the former being referred to Mercury and the latter to the higher aspected Sol. Thus we see matters in their formative stage, as Mercury represents the starting point for the ascent to Sol. Mercury is the messenger of the gods and symbolises those processes which we know as logical thought. The overall theme is therefore one of progress achieved through careful deliberation with perhaps that little bit of luck that tips the scales in our favour.

---

9 in 11

Correspondences
Yesod, 'Foundation'; Luna. The Zodiacal Sign of Aquarius, the Water-bearer; Tarot Trump XVII 'The Star'.
   Luna rules the element Air; Aquarius is of Air.

Main Principle   Luna in Atu XVII 'The Star'.

The Title   Providential chance.

The Reading

The Universe is filled with beginnings and endings, creations and destructions. Every ending marks a new beginning; each act of creation marks the end of destruction. This is the eternal dance of the stars in the body of the great cosmic entity.

Every man and every woman is a star; each is a shining soul within the body of the great cosmic entity. The will of the Universe, the movement of change and progress, is reflected by every soul on earth. Light increases and diminishes; the achievements of man advance or remain still. Progress is achieved by degrees.

Here we observe the opening of the Universe in growth. The eternal dance of the stars continues afresh; light now increases upon the earth.

Inspiration springs up from deep wells; the seeker of progress drinks of the waters thereof and proceeds with increased advantage. Insight opens the doorways to worthy opportunity; beneficial gains are obtained from providential chance.

Darkness quickly recedes. Light from the higher sheds illumination on the lower. The seeker of progress advances and rejoices in the fruits of the firmament and the land.

Notes

The dual nature of Luna is here seen in its positive aspect; growth or waxing strong instead of decreasing or waning. The celestial body of Luna increases the light from the Star (Tarot Trump XVII) as a lens increases light from the Sun. In this instance the sterile nature of Air is transformed into a productive force through its ability to instil new breath and vitality into a stale circumstance.

The statement 'Every man and every woman is a star' first appeared in Liber Al vel Legis (The Book of The Law), which Aleister Crowley received by way of direct transmission from a disembodied Intelligence of considerable power.

---

3 in 12

Correspondences
Binah, 'Understanding'; Saturn. The Zodiacal Sign of Pisces, the Fishes; Tarot Trump XVIII 'The Moon'.

Saturn rules the element Water; Pisces is of Water.

Main Principle   Saturn in Atu XVIII 'The Moon'.

The Title   Constraint.

The Reading

When the stream of life grows indolent, and jackals prowl the gloomy byways in search of unwary souls, the traveller on the Path to light should advance with infinite care, taking cautious steps appropriate to the times.

Progress under conditions of oppression or constraint is made by one who adopts movement relevant to circumstance. Knowledge of the ever-changing phases of the Universe brings great comfort; darkness must yield to light. That which is obscured must be revealed when the dark phase is done.

Here we observe a time of great darkness. Uncertainty will rise up and distort the appearance of all things. Jackals will approach.

Adversaries who prowl as jackals are despatched by denying them substance for their greed. By advancing with infinite care one may destroy the efforts of unworthy enemies and render them impotent.

Uncertainty is vanquished when the will to proceed is fixed and iron-rigid. Unbending determination accompanied by watchful awareness will here lead to small success. The oppression or constraint now clustered in the darkness will be held at bay if continuous caution is exercised.

Notes

Tarot Trump XVIII is one of the least auspicious cards in that its Path traverses one of the darkest recesses of the Tree of Life. It is the Path of illusion, deceit and danger. The entrance of Saturn indicates a measure of beneficial control exerted over these negative forces. Saturn is slow to move but powerful in effect; these qualities will be reflected in the manner with which events are seen to progress.

---

4 in 1

Correspondences

Chesed, 'Mercy'; Jupiter. The Zodiacal Sign of Aries, the Ram; Tarot Trump IV 'The Emperor'.

Jupiter rules the element Water; Aries is of Fire.

Main Principle   Jupiter in Atu IV 'The Emperor'.

The Title   Careful husbandry.

The Reading

The Emperor is in a benevolent mood. He sees wealth and abundance all about him in the palace, and vows to give much to the needy of his Empire. There will be rejoicing in humble quarters at the Emperor's generosity.

But when the royal wealth is distributed and spent, the Emperor must realise that he has at the last only himself to give. How then will the poor who have tasted transitory wealth accustom themselves to a return to poverty? How will they regard their Emperor who has lifted them up to an empty height, and can at the last offer only himself?

If the Emperor would create lasting benefits within his Empire, he must establish the means of continual growth.

By careful planning through the seasons, the harvest will be reaped in proportion to the seed. Thus the small becomes great; there is no dissipation and loss of the original sum. One seed at planting may yield ten at harvest. Continual growth is made possible; there is no return to poverty.

The benevolent Emperor now stands at the threshold of a new cycle. The Omens indicate abundance. But lasting prosperity throughout the realm is assured only through careful husbandry.

It is the Emperor's natural inclination to make a grand and munificent gesture, though it is far better for his people to receive steady increase born of wisdom than a large and sudden share of folly.

Notes

Jupiter is an immensely powerful force and could easily overwhelm the character of the Emperor. This is because Aries is a Cardinal Sign, the fires of which are new born and have yet to achieve stability. But Jupiter is 4, the essence of form, and so presents a firm foundation to an otherwise fluctuating condition. The problem stems from the Emperor, who is quite likely to over-react to Jupiter's magnificence and squander the benefits thereof.

5 in 2

Correspondences
Geburah, 'Strength'; Mars. The Zodiacal Sign of Taurus, the Bull; Tarot Trump V 'The Hierophant'.
Mars rules the element Fire; Taurus is of Earth.

Main Principle   Mars in Atu V 'The Hierophant'.

The Title   Exaggerated enthusiasm.

The Reading

The Hierophant abandons his patience and composure. Filled with the desire to advance his progress he engages himself feverishly in many tasks. Calling upon his god and companions he incites activity in all the spheres. With unbecoming industry he proceeds in the pursuit of success.

Such impetuous actions do not serve to win praiseworthy achievement. The high office of Hierophant is served with serenity, deliberation, steadiness and control. Restraint is necessary when responsibility is great; exaggerated enthusiasm will lead to regret.

Activity in all the spheres will result in the loss of balanced endeavour; reduced coordination transforms harmony into chaos. Impetuous actions will give rise to harmful error; grief is encountered where patience is diminished.

The Hierophant now walks a path set with hazards; he approaches pitfalls of his own making.

The desire to force the advance of progress will result in decline. The Hierophant will lose the respect of his disciples; they will seek another master.

Returning to the conduct proper to his calling will stay the effects of folly. Continued impetuosity will bring great misfortune.

Notes

Mars has little to commend it when placed in the Path of Tarot Trump V. The warrior nature of Mars – even its boundless energy and enthusiasm – can bring little advantage to one who clearly ought to move with serenity and restraint. The fires of Mars fairly scorch the earth of Taurus; it is a heat which is too fierce to bring forth any growth. Indeed, anything which is in the early stages of germination is likely to be destroyed.

6 in 3

Correspondences
Tiphareth, 'Beauty'; Sol. The Zodiacal Sign of Gemini, the Twins; Tarot Trump VI 'The Lovers'.

Sol rules the element Air; Gemini is of Air.

Main Principle   Sol in Atu VI 'The Lovers'.

The Title   Discarding.

The Reading

The desire to create beneficial change springs from dissatisfaction. When all things yield pleasure and bring satisfaction, change is neither actively sought nor required. But when pleasure and satisfaction are no longer obtained from familiar things they are discarded and replaced. When dissatisfaction is found with that which is already of great worth, we see aspiration leading to great endeavour.

Here we observe the emergence of desires arising to claim a distant and exalted goal. Therefore we see the beginnings of great endeavour, and the discarding of established habits. The quest begins from a position of great advantage, so also do we see the discarding of things of value.

When things of worth are left behind in the search for progress in new directions we see courage and convictions guiding each step of the journey. When this occurs from a position of advantage, which could have been won only through intelligent and diligent application, the journey will not have been undertaken without forethought and so presages success and good fortune. This will justify all preceding deeds.

The emergence of desire is the rising up of the Self in its need. When the Self encourages great endeavour and brings later achievement the seeker draws closer to enduring satisfaction.

Notes

Tarot Trump VI occupies the 17th Path between Tiphareth and Binah, and so represents a fairly advanced stage of attainment. The present domination of Tiphareth (as Sol) indicates that the exalted reaches of Binah have yet to be won, but are nonetheless within view and generate a desire to proceed with the upward climb. It is the will to advance beyond what has been accomplished previously, and portends success.

7 in 4

Correspondences
Netzach, 'Victory'; Venus. The Zodiacal Sign of Cancer, the Crab;
Tarot Trump VII 'The Chariot'.

Venus rules the element Fire; Cancer is of Water.

Main Principle Venus in Atu VII 'The Chariot'.

The Title Remain loyal.

The Reading

When the Charioteer is accepted into the ranks of the great army, it is
clearly his chosen duty to reflect the will of those in high command.

Having once entered into his commitment the Charioteer must abide
by the consequences of his decision.

The Charioteer now has before him a journey of importance. He will
ensure that his chariot and steeds are competent to perform the task
ahead. Such elementary precautions are vital if the journey is not to end
in grief.

As emissary of his army, the Charioteer is representative of all that
they are. Thus he will be subjected to the closest scrutiny by those
destined to receive him. The responsibility of his task may, therefore,
evoke feelings of doubt and fear. Matters of great importance are rarely
approached without trepidation.

Even before he passes through the gates of his own city, the Charioteer
may feel panic stirring within his breast. He may be inclined to abandon
his army and the burden they have placed upon him.

But the Charioteer must consider that the army is that of his own
choosing, and they in their turn have vested in him their highest faith. He
should further consider that important tasks are not placed in the hands
of unworthy servants.

The duty of the Charioteer is clear; he must remain loyal to his army
and reflect their will. To abandon one cause for the employ of another
would not bring salvation. Great generals do not admire the capricious
or the weak.

The Charioteer will succeed on his journey if he adheres to what is
right.

Notes

The exalted position of Tarot Trump VII on the Tree of Life insulates it, to a degree, from external influence, but Venus can and does employ devious strategies to snare the unwary. The Charioteer may therefore be tempted by a siren song to seek an easier and seemingly more pleasant existence away from his Path; but the Charioteer is subservient to Binah, and this disciplined sphere is well above the authority of that occupied by Venus.

---

8 in 5

Correspondences
Hod, 'Glory'; Mercury. The Zodiacal Sign of Leo, the Lion; Tarot Trump XI 'Lust'.
  Mercury rules the element Water; Leo is of Fire.

Main Principle   Mercury in Atu XI 'Lust'.

The Title   United creativity.

The Reading

The naked woman rides astride the mighty lion. Strength and mercy are held in balance; progress is made on the Path to attainment.
  Harmony must exist between beast and rider if their union is to continue and their journey succeed. Such harmony can be secured only through the successful combination of strength and mercy. The lion could devour its rider; savage strength could overwhelm the useful quality of mercy. By attending to the business of maintaining balanced order, the woman and the lion have assured themselves continued progress.
  With balanced order firmly established the woman and the lion remain free to contemplate the journey ahead. By engaging themselves in united creativity directed towards a common goal, obstacles on the Path will be overcome swiftly.
  The union of opposites, such as woman and beast, brings great knowledge and bestows authority: the combination of extremes dissolves apparent duality and reveals the heart of the One divine. This leads to a recognition of truth.

When a journey proceeds in balanced order and is directed by knowledge which encompasses the divine, no troublesome resistance to progress can endure. With the added vitality of united creativity to aid them, the woman and the lion will advance to great heights.

Notes

Mercury is the messenger of the gods; his effect upon the beast and rider of Tarot Trump XI is highly beneficial. He makes the third point of an incomplete triangle; it is the formation of a harmonic trinity. The watery nature of Mercury is curiously compatible with the fire of Leo. It is the surging force of water married to the leaping force of fire. The outcome is an upward thrust of combined elements which, as a result of their combining together, have transmuted into a higher and finer form. The natural consequence is a progression towards the exalted state of Perfection itself.

---

9 in 6

Correspondences
Yesod, 'Foundation'; Luna. The Zodiacal Sign of Virgo, the Virgin; Tarot Trump IX 'The Hermit'.
   Luna rules the element Air; Virgo is of Earth.

Main Principle   Luna in Atu IX 'The Hermit'.

The Title   Necessity of withdrawal.

The Reading

The Hermit withdraws into the peace and solitude of the hermitage that he may achieve attainment. The benefits of solitude may lead to considerable progress on the Path.
   Here we observe the Hermit who realises the necessity of withdrawal. The times are such that journeying in the outside world would not bring him any advantage. The phase of useful activity is done; now is the time for thoughtful contemplation.

By withdrawing into the hermitage and refraining from external activity the Hermit will be free to organise the elements of his world into their proper place. The absence of distraction will allow him to attend to the important task of contemplation. Through contemplation the hermit will view his position in the universal plan with great clarity.

Assessment and rearrangement are necessary when the processes of life become disorganised. Through undisturbed contemplation it is possible to discover the root of the breakdown of order. The means of starting anew is then revealed.

When the process of analysis is complete the Hermit will be free to leave the hermitage. He will leave in a position of great strength and advantage. Until then it is better for him to refrain from activity, and attend instead to the contemplation of his position in the ebb and flow of his life's directing current.

Notes

Luna entering the Path of Tarot Trump IX can produce a tendency to indulge in deep analysis. Thus the Hermit is seen to withdraw from the outside world and engage himself accordingly. This is due to airy Luna, with its powerful visionary qualities, permeating the empty soil of Virgo and awakening in the latter a deep-seated awareness of universal order. This is a process which must occur before any real progress on the Path is achieved. It is the arousal of the barren matter prior to the act of fertilisation.

---

3 in 7

Correspondences
Binah, 'Understanding'; Saturn. The Zodiacal Sign of Libra, the Balances; Tarot Trump VIII 'Adjustment'.

Saturn rules the element Water; Libra is of Air.

Main Principle   Saturn in Atu VIII 'Adjustment'.

The Title   Regulated order.

The Reading

The Universe reaches perfection by balancing strength against weakness. Such action demands the assistance of firm and rigid law.

With strength balanced against weakness a state of harmony is achieved; through harmony the foundations are laid for the attainment of perfection. Furtherance of the law of Adjustment will lead to such attainment.

Adjustment is the process employed by Nature to achieve its equilibrium. Weak and strong, stress and conflict are arranged in fine balance one against the other. The result is the tranquility of equilibrium. In this way explosive chaos yields to regulated order throughout the Universe above and below.

Here we observe the law of adjustment being served with firm and meticulous rigidity. Unbalanced elements are directed into balance; deviating forces are refined with calm precision. Order is established with inexorable assiduity.

When the law of Adjustment is served with such unyielding diligence great progress is made. The Universe above and below then moves with a regulated and predictable exactitude.

All the elements are in their rightful place; events proceed satisfactorily under strict and intelligent management.

Notes

The nature of Saturn is suited perfectly to the requirements of Libra and Tarot Trump VIII. The qualities of discipline and limitation are vital to the successful creation of balanced works. The underlying inference here is that firm control will be exerted beneficially over those matters which now require attention.

---

4 in 8

Correspondences
Chesed, 'Mercy'; Jupiter. The Zodiacal Sign of Scorpio, the Scorpion; Tarot Trump XIII 'Death'.

Jupiter rules the element Water; Scorpio is of Water.

Main Principle   Jupiter in Atu XIII 'Death'.

The Title   Remorse will follow.

The Reading

It is the avowed duty of the Reaper to cut down the obstacles to his attainment on the Path. In accordance with his duty he proceeds to make clear his way to future progress.

Careless action by one who wields a scythe will result in grief. Progress is achieved when the unworthy is cut down, or when the harvest gathered is ripe and ready. Grief is encountered when the worthy is cut down with the unworthy, or when the unripe harvest is gathered along with the ripe.

Here we observe the Reaper failing to exercise caution in his affairs. In proceeding to make clear his way to future progress he has brought down his scythe upon every upstanding thing. Remorse will follow.

The Reaper has been overwhelmed by the nature of his task. Careless, and drunk with the power he wields, he has extended his actions to encompass all things. The worthy has been cut down with the unworthy. At the final stroke of his scythe he will encounter a world of desolation, ruin and decay. He will mourn for the passing of useful resources.

Until the final stroke is made there is opportunity for reprieve. The raised blade should not fall again until an enquiry is made of all circumstances leading to the present. Future progress will then be achieved through an understanding of the errors of the past.

Notes

The regal nature of Jupiter is misplaced in the Path of Tarot Trump XIII. The exalted Jupiterian qualities are alien to the Path; the figure represented by the Trump cannot accommodate the forces without a struggle. The waters of Jupiter and Scorpio combine to produce an almost uncontrollable flood. The word *almost* is significant, for this is not an absolute state. With suitable caution the flood-waters can still be reduced to manageable proportions, and circumstances brought under control.

---

5 in 9

Correspondences

Geburah, 'Strength'; Mars. The Zodiacal Sign of Sagittarius, the Archer; Tarot Trump XIV 'Art'.

Mars rules the element Fire; Sagittarius is of Fire.

Main Principle   Mars in Atu XIV 'Art'.

The Title   Contention and disturbance.

The Reading

The existence of the Universe is maintained through the natural balance between the forces of creation and destruction. When creation and destruction are weighed in equal measure there is neither loss nor gain, but a state of eternal Being. Thus the Infinite can neither increase nor decrease, and the soul of the Universe remains eternal.

When creation and destruction remain in equilibrium there is a state of harmony in the Universe. When one seeks to advance on the other a displacement is created which echoes throughout the entire cosmic entity.

Here we observe the origins of such displacement.

The world of Man is subservient to Universal law, therefore when opposing forces of equal measure within one's own realm enter into contention there will be appropriate widespread disturbance. This is manifested as great and restless activity. But there can be neither increase nor decrease.

Contention between two equal forces cannot be resolved in victory. Thus the wise man seeks to avoid contention by maintaining a sense of balance in all his affairs.

Great and restless activity will serve no useful purpose; a desirable objective is achieved through steady and consistent application. Tranquil and enduring progress is impossible in the presence of contention and disturbance.

Notes

The activity represented by Tarot Trump XIV is one of synthesis, the joining of compatible elements in a process of refinement. It is an operation of love under the direction of a controlled will. The introduction of the aggressive qualities of Mars into the proceedings results in conflict. The operation is ruined and aborted. The fires of Mars, when added to the fires of Sagittarius, produce a blaze that consumes without refining, which is against the objective illustrated by the trump.

6 in 10

Correspondences
Tiphareth, 'Beauty'; Sol. The Zodiacal Sign of Capricorn, the Goat; Tarot Trump XV 'The Devil'.
Sol rules the element Air; Capricorn is of Earth.

Main Principle   Sol in Atu XV 'The Devil'.

The Title   Practical effort.

The Reading

The great Mountain Goat stands sure-footed and triumphant upon the high peak. The arduous slopes have been vanquished; success is achieved through steady endeavour.

Here we observe the pinnacle attained after difficulty. Practical effort and disciplined steps serve to win the distant object of desire.

As the Mountain Goat upon the peak is above all other beasts, so are all seekers of success raised up in dignity and authority when victory is won through endeavour.

Practical effort and disciplined steps are required when the Path ahead climbs steeply upward. Determination and aspiration are vital at such a time. If descent to the lowlands is to be avoided the arduous slopes must be traversed and conquered.

Persistence on the upward Path brings steady ascent. The retreat of observable horizons brings new opportunity into view; increased dignity and authority will command benefit and advantage from newly discovered quarters.

When the great Mountain Goat commands the high peak, lesser creatures yield to his magnificence and majesty. Assault on one in a position of advantage is not undertaken lightly.

Notes

On the Tree of Life Trump XV occupies the 26th Path between Hod, 'Glory', and Tiphareth, 'Beauty'; Hod being the lower aspected of the two spheres. As Tiphareth is now the predominant force the indication is that the journey from the lower has been (or will be) successfully accomplished. Hod is the sphere of intellect and reason; the inference is that victory arises from carefully planned action rather than chance.

7 in 11

Correspondences
Netzach, 'Victory'; Venus. The Zodiacal Sign of Aquarius, the Water-bearer; Tarot Trump XVII 'The Star'.

Venus rules the element Fire; Aquarius is of Air.

Main Principle   Venus in Atu XVII 'The Star'.

The Title   New alliances.

The Reading

Here the higher fills the lower with the desire to create. New alliances come in unusual ways; it is as if the dove and the raven are singing together.

Creativity rises and brings the will to transform. When the will to transform is present, established order yields willingly to advantageous change. But where creativity is not disciplined a vision of achievement may obscure surrounding reality. Such visions produce impractical schemes. Change is then resisted; the obstacles of practicality are not overcome with ease.

If progress is now to be achieved, the desire to create must be directed with intelligence. The building up of advantage from worthy opportunity meets with success when reality is acknowledged.

Creativity inspires unusual action. This leads to new alliances of surprising combination. The dove and the raven are alike yet dissimilar; working together brings them mutual advantage and encouragement. Obstacles which cannot be surmounted by one are vanquished with assistance. But obstacles that are clearly warnings of foolish endeavour should not be challenged.

Notes

Venus entering the Path of Tarot Trump XVII serves to create an over-optimistic point of view. There is a tendency to view the world through rose-coloured glasses. It is the jubilant enthusiasm of a child ill-equipped to deal with the complexities of life. The Reading suggests that a potential for success definitely exists, but due safeguards must be employed. The dove and the raven are birds referred to Venus; they represent the gentle, if sometimes dark, beauty of that sphere.

8 in 12

Correspondences
Hod, 'Glory'; Mercury. The Zodiacal Sign of Pisces, the Fishes; Tarot
Trump XVIII 'The Moon'.
Mercury rules the element Water; Pisces is of Water.

Main Principle   Mercury in Atu XVIII 'The Moon'.

The Title   Deception.

The Reading

The reverse of wisdom is folly; therefore, when the Path ahead is eaten
through with the vermin of folly, the seeker ascends not to wisdom, but
descends to a world where all is awry.

Progress through life, as on the Path itself, is achieved by looking to
the high peaks of attainment and proceeding in a manner favourable to
success. But when all that can be seen is inverted or reversed; when
trickery and deceit are seen to usurp the place of wisdom itself, grave and
deadly misfortune abounds. Progress cannot be achieved.

Here we observe the madness of deception run riot. Nothing is as it
seems; all is distortion.

When grave and deadly misfortune abound the seeker must swiftly
withdraw. No advantage can be gained by remaining and offering
resistance.

In the silence of withdrawal consideration should be given to the cause
of such folly. The severing of old ties is favourable.

By adopting the company of wiser elders, the student on the Path
gains useful knowledge of the correct manner of ascent.

Notes

Mercury is particularly ill-dignified in Pisces. This is illustrated in the
above reading, where the perverse nature of the corresponding Tarot
trump brings out the worst possible Mercurial traits. Instead of the
winged messenger of the gods, we see the rambling and shifty Ape of
Unreason. Divine influence no longer has the upper hand. The position
of the trump on the Tree of Life, and the fact that Mercury is a youthful
god, together suggest the folly of inexperience, the stumblings of the
student blind in the dark.

9 in 1

Correspondences
Yesod, 'Foundation'; Luna. The Zodiacal Sign of Aries, the Ram; Tarot Trump IV 'The Emperor'.

Luna rules the element Air; Aries is of Fire.

Main Principle   Luna in Atu IV 'The Emperor'.

The Title   Unsteady.

The Reading

The young Emperor who wishes to advance the well-being of his Empire should proceed with steady caution. Inconsiderate or inconsistant action will not bring lasting benefit.

The young Emperor is concerned to establish himself as a leader. But he cannot reveal his potential to the full; he has yet to learn the complexities of government. The changeable enthusiasm of youth is incompatible with the consistency required for matters of state; the young Emperor must heed the counsel of advisors before effecting change.

The Empire itself is stable; there is no threat from hostile forces. In times of peace, leaders are free to contemplate their visions of progress and achievement. The young Emperor now entertains such visions, but he lacks the consistency of maturity to bring them to fruition. He is unsteady and changeable in his approach.

If he sincerely wishes to advance the well-being of his Empire, the young Emperor must learn to proceed steadily with carefully developed plans. Inconsiderate or inconsistant action will not bring him the success he desires.

The Empire will decline under the leadership of one who is prone to changeable enthusiasm, if he does not heed wise counsel.

Notes

Aries is a Cardinal Sign and as such represents the first swift outpourings of fire. Thus the Emperor of Atu IV is as yet inexperienced, even potentially unstable. The gross and powerful energies of Luna easily disperse the young flame in all directions, leaving the Emperor weakened and at a marked disadvantage.

8 in 10

Correspondences

Binah, 'Understanding'; Saturn. The Zodiacal Sign of Taurus, the Bull;
Tarot Trump V 'The Hierophant'.
   Saturn rules the element Water; Taurus is of Earth.

Main Principle   Saturn in Atu V 'The Hierophant'.

The Title   Forthcoming transition.

The Reading

The Hierophant perceives the resplendant City beyond the divide; he
progresses toward exalted attainment.

Those who cross the waiting divide are stripped of all that they are.
Their sacrifice brings reward through exchange, for in the yielding up of
themselves they are established in the realm of the divine. This is success
in the Great Work. It is the goal which the Hierophant so ardently seeks.

Thus new order is obtained at the cost of the old. Progress now brings
welcome change and transformation.

The Hierophant now orders his affairs to prepare for his great
attainment. By setting aside what is no longer required he encourages the
approach of good fortune. The maintenance of obsolete possessions will
merely hinder the establishment of new order.

Those in the Hierophant's charge will benefit from his forthcoming
transition. His authority and ability increase as he now advances; he
brings stability and comfort to those who look to him in their need.

The Path chosen now brings its high reward. Attainment of the new in
return for the giving up of the old will recompense all labour spent in
preparing the way for change.

Notes

Saturn is above the Abyss, the gulf that divides the noumenal (or the
ideal) from the actual world of appearance and form. The entrance of
Saturn into the Path of the Hierophant indicates that an ideal state is
about to be achieved (as opposed to *the* ideal, which is a mystical state
beyond the reach of all but a few).

The exalted nature of Saturn's waters give sustenance to the earth of
Taurus; the Hierophant, accordingly, increases in stature. It is the
culmination and reward for past efforts, the manifestation of a long-
pursued goal.

4 in 3

Correspondences
Chesed, 'Mercy'; Jupiter. The Zodiacal Sign of Gemini, the Twins; Tarot Trump VI 'The Lovers'.
   Jupiter rules the element Water; Gemini is of Air.

Main Principle   Jupiter in Atu VI 'The Lovers'.

The Title   Accomplished works.

The Reading

One who is versed in one art alone will not proceed beyond the limitations of his chosen sphere, even though his skills increase. But one who is adaptable to many arts and performs them in an accomplished manner will find such adaptability of inestimable value in obtaining success from diverse opportunities.

Here we observe adaptable intelligence and practical creativity establishing itself through accomplished works. This will bring good fortune. New acquaintances come forth; there is activity and increase in many spheres.

The threads that link all things in their diversity will be gathered up; from them will be composed a new creation that transforms diversity into unified splendour. The many will become the one; the one shall become the prime occupation of its creator. It will be the supreme culmination of all past endeavours. Diverse and minor success becomes one superior success; lesser fortune becomes great.

This is the reward for one who is adaptable to many arts, and performs them in an accomplished manner.

Notes

Jupiter represents an immensely powerful stabilising force; also abundance and magnificence. When Jupiter appears in the Path of Tarot Trump VI these qualities are, in part, manifested therein. Thus the process of unification, as illustrated by the trump, finds all the resources necessary to meet with success; things fall into place with an agreeable ease and convenience.

5 in 4

Correspondences
Geburah, 'Strength'; Mars. The Zodiacal Sign of Cancer, the Crab; Tarot Trump VII 'The Chariot'.

Mars rules the element Fire; Cancer is of Water.

Main Principle   Mars in Atu VII 'The Chariot'.

The Title   Brilliance of a comet.

The Reading

The Charioteer is fully armed within his chariot of war. He is clad in warrior's armour; he glitters with magnificent fires of unrestrained fury.

All the elements are in their rightful place. Great achievements are made through the successful employment of an engine of war.

Here we observe the Charioteer executing his duty with great skill and vigour. The Path has been chosen well. All obstacles will fall; the objective will be achieved.

With his battle cry upon his lips the Charioteer proceeds; he thus proclaims his intentions to all around him. He passes all other mortals as the dazzling brilliance of a comet passes over a world in darkness.

The Charioteer cannot fail in his mission. He leaves the known to engage the unknown, but such is his skill and vigour that he will endure where others fall.

By asserting his strength he will win the esteem and compliance of those in the land he now seeks; honours will be given to his name.

Notes

Tarot Trump VII descends from Binah to the fifth Sephirah Geburah. The Understanding of Binah thus reaches down to Geburah via the mediation of the Charioteer. The sphere of Mars is the Charioteer's first stop in his quest; it is his destined point of arrival. Thus the controlling forces of Binah serve to turn the violent and aggressive qualities of Mars to good effect and prepare the way for further progress.

6 in 5

Correspondences
Tiphareth, 'Beauty'; Sol. The Zodiacal Sign of Leo, the Lion; Tarot Trump XI 'Lust'.

Sol rules the element Air; Leo is of Fire.

Main Principle   Sol in Atu XI 'Lust'.

The Title   Released desire.

The Reading

Here we observe the formation of a strong uniting bond between two opposites, each possessing noble and honourable characteristics. Therefore we witness the origins of truly great works.

When two opposites each possess the qualities of nobility and honour, we see elements which are not dissimilar by virtue of their strength or weakness, but by virtue of their appearance. Thus the outward appearance serves to disguise an inner truth. The revealing of this inner truth to facilitate the forming of a bond indicates the coming of a moment of destiny, the fruition of planned intention.

This will confer great success. When inner truths are so revealed and brought together we see the discarding of the shield of prudence for the freedom of realization. From this flows works of great worth and achievement, for the unrestricted activity of the revealed Self (which is truth) creates changes which are wholly in accord with its released desire.

Such changes will lead to important and agreeable rearrangements in established order. There will be a guided and inspired reconstruction of life's deteriorating patterns. The separate will be made one; the two will be joined.

It is a time of joyful satisfaction.

Notes

Sol reaches its Dignity in Leo, and is wholly at home in the Path of Tarot Trump XI. The unifying aspect of Sol here operates to its fullest limit; the opposites symbolised in the trump (woman and lion) are brought together in total harmony. The result is good fortune and success.

7 in 6

Correspondences
Netzach, 'Victory'; Venus. The Zodiacal Sign of Virgo, the Virgin; Tarot
Trump IX 'The Hermit'.
   Venus rules the element Fire; Virgo is of Earth.

Main Principle   Venus in Atu IX 'The Hermit'.

The Title   Leaving the hermitage.

The Reading

Consideration of the ways to success brings advantage to one who has
the will to transform understanding into appropriate deeds.

   Progress towards success is made when conflict is absent. Harmony
encourages the placid arrangement of useful resources into their most
beneficial order. Conflict hinders such activity; progress is arrested in
the pursuit of calm.

   When the Hermit knows of the ways to success yet remains cloistered
in his cell, there is conflict between understanding and deed. The
conveniences of the hermitage restrain the quest for success in other
spheres. Abiding in the hermitage does not remove the awareness of the
potential that exists beyond familiar walls.

   By leaving the hermitage and engaging the cooperation of helpful
companions the hermit will now turn understanding into appropriate
deeds.

   The arrangement of useful resources into beneficial order will be made
possible; unworthy conflict of interests will then no longer stay the
hermit from success.

   Harmony will be established in the absence of conflict; happiness will
justify abandoning the familiar for new and more challenging pursuits.

Notes

Venus inspires a vision of beauty. This is of little benefit to the Hermit of
Tarot Trump IX if he remains in isolation. The rose-glow of Venus
warms the waiting soil of Virgo; the conditions are ripe for planting. If
one wishes to contemplate one's reasons for the lack of progress, or
formulate plans for advancement, isolation can be of advantage. But
once one has seen the light it is advisable to summon up courage and put
the theory into practice.

8 in 7

Correspondences ·
Hod, 'Glory'; Mercury. The Zodiacal Sign of Libra, the Balances; Tarot Trump VIII 'Adjustment'.
  Mercury rules the element Water; Libra is of Air.

Main Principle Mercury in Atu VIII 'Adjustment'.

The Title Sacrifices of progress.

The Reading

The seeker of perfection orders his life according to the ebb and flow of the universal tides, so creating harmony between his movements below and the greater movements above. Desirable advance is then achieved.

  Adjustment is necessary when that which is below is in conflict with the greater movements above. Incorrect adjustment brings greater conflict. But when the higher and lower are brought together in concord there is cause for great rejoicing. Desirable advance approaches.

  Here we observe the seeker who perceives the need for change, and carries out adjustment with precise and diligent trial. The elements are ordered into their rightful occupations; all things proceed towards perfection.

  Great progress is made by one who so readily follows the dictates of balance. For the achievement of harmony is the achievement of balance, wherein life is so ordered that conflict is avoided between hostile extremes.

  All advance is purchased at the cost of the present; the achievement of concord demands loss in proportion to the gain. This is the law of the balances of adjustment. The dedicated seeker proceeds with the necessary adjustments knowing that the pain of sacrifice is nought, and the reward of achievement all. The casting out of the worthless in the pursuit of excellence is a labour hard and tormenting, for the sacrifices of progress are supreme.

Notes

Mercury entering the Path of Tarot Trump VIII brings cold but precise thought to bear on the issues in hand. This attitude is vital if the correct decisions are to be made. The reading suggests that matters are about to proceed in exactly this manner, with the result that the objective will be secured at all costs. Mercury is thoroughly cold blooded in his approach, but the end usually justifies the means.

9 in 8

Correspondences
Yesod, 'Foundation'; Luna. The Zodiacal Sign of Scorpio, the Scorpion;
Tarot Trump XIII 'Death'.
   Luna rules the element Air; Scorpio is of Water.

Main Principle   Luna in Atu XIII 'Death'.

The Title   No harvest.

The Reading

Spirit descends into matter and returns to Spirit; the Universe evolves
from chaos, establishes order and returns to chaos. The pulse of the
cosmic entity ebbs and flows; Aeons are born, Aeons die.
   The cessation of one cycle is always the birth of another. With every
ending throughout the Universe there is the beginning of a new phase.
Time flows unceasingly; in the flowing of time change must occur.
   By observing the phases of growth and decay the wise man knows
when to advance or remain still, as the Reaper knows when to reap the
harvest or abide in his quarters.
   Here we observe the cessation of a cycle. A phase of Fortune's tide
proceeds towards its lowest ebb. There is no harvest for the Reaper. He
remains patiently within his quarters.
   At the ending of a cycle one must count the lessons learned, the
benefits won and lost. Without such comprehension of achievements
and defeats one cannot receive the ever-coming cycle with advantage.
   The wise man now bides his time, recounting the past to good effect.
When the new cycle blossoms in its season there will be much to be
accomplished.

Notes

On the Tree of Life Luna and the Sephira Yesod represent the
penultimate stage of the descent of Spirit into gross matter. Tarot Trump
XIII represents a complex process of change. These two elements in
combination serve to indicate that matters are now approaching their
lowest level. But the Universe does not stagnate. One phase or stage
inevitably follows its predecessor, just as Kether, 'The Crown',
inevitably follows Malkuth in the circle of change.

3 in 9

Correspondences
Binah, 'Understanding'; Saturn. The Zodiacal Sign of Sagittarius, the Archer; Tarot Trump XIV 'Art'.

Saturn rules the element Water; Sagittarius is of Fire.

Main Principle   Saturn in Atu XIV 'Art'.

The Title   Patience and thoroughness.

The Reading

The Universe moves serenely through the centuries, obtaining order out of chaos through the unhurried movement of elements into their proper rank, unmindful of the passage of the years.

The seeker on the Path to attainment observes the unhurried movements above and endeavours to accomplish his will in a similar manner.

Here we observe the successful advance of one who acts in accord with the unhurried movements of the Universe. The absence of undue haste will lead to progress through success born of thoroughness.

By attending to the task of completing each step on the Path in a thorough and patient fashion, worthy and lasting progress is achieved. Haste does not by itself secure rapid gain. Advance is achieved through success. Success is determined by thoroughness. One who proceeds in a thorough and unhurried manner will advance with greater certainty than one who acts with impetuous speed.

When the need for patience and thoroughness is so clearly marked, so too is the presence of danger. The studious observation of every circumstance will yield knowledge of concealed or latent peril. The unmasking of definite adversity permits the avoidance of grief.

Notes

The steadying and restricting qualities of Saturn serve to correct the impetuous Sagittarian nature. The effect is reflected via Tarot Trump XIV where the alchemical or unifying processes there indicated are provided with the calm necessary for success in the operation. The transmutation of the lower into the higher is allowed to proceed in a manner destined to yield the best possible results.

4 in 10

Correspondences
Chesed, 'Mercy'; Jupiter. The Zodiacal Sign of Capricorn, the Goat; Tarot Trump XV 'The Devil'.
Jupiter rules the element Water; Capricorn is of Earth.

Main Principle   Jupiter in Atu XV 'The Devil'.

The Title   Danger of stumbling.

The Reading

The Mountain Goat has grown fat through indulgence. He can no longer negotiate the slopes with safety. He is in danger of stumbling. It is the proper nature of the Mountain Goat to ascend the slopes as he wills, nimbly and with deft precision. When normal order is disturbed by foolish action grief will be encountered. No progress will be made.

The Mountain Goat has strayed from his rightful path. Indulgence in matters which cannot further progress are of no value; even danger may lurk within. Turning aside from what is required leads to unfounded happiness. The pursuit of what is out of place brings useless change. Unfounded happiness and useless change combine in dangerous allegiance; the unavoidable discovery of folly brings swift retribution.

Progress is achieved when intention and action join together in the meritorious pursuit of worthy goals. By maintaining the necessary mobility of mind and body the Mountain Goat remains nimble; he does not stumble, neither does he succumb to the swift dartings of predators.

The seeker of life's Path observes the virtue of being true to kind, and understands that all things must stand in their allotted order and status.

Notes

The grand, expansive nature of Jupiter is something of a trap for the lonely leaper of the heights as represented by Tarot Trump XV. Jupiter is 4, the essence of form and stability; but Jupiter is also the 'vision of God face to face', a highly exalted state to which the lower aspected trump is not yet equal. It is a position too far removed, too ambitious a leap. There is a danger of an inflation of the ego leading to a false sense of importance.

5 in 11

Correspondences
Geburah, 'Strength'; Mars. The Zodiacal Sign of Aquarius, the Water-bearer; Tarot Trump XVII 'The Star'.

Mars rules the element Fire; Aquarius is of Air.

Main Principle   Mars in Atu XVII 'The Star'.

The Title   Contradiction.

The Reading

The desire to bring about useful change, the inspiration to transform potential into achievement, can not be brought to a successful conclusion when activity and inertia alternate, bringing first advance and progress, then decline and dissipation, as when a cart is pushed up a hill then allowed to lose ground when the driving force is withdrawn.

Here we observe the star that shines and is dimmed; it is as the cart that advances and retreats. No progress is made. The expenditure of great effort achieves no advance away from the point of departure.

Forces now operate in marked opposition. The desire to bring about useful change is met with contradiction. Anxiety will arise and add to confusion.

Clearly the elements are misplaced. There is no harmony, no coming together of things useful to progress. Contradiction leads to sending forth and retaliation; Decline and dissipation will follow; the elements will resolve into chaos.

When contradiction stems from companions or society, the change desired is manifestly unwelcome. When contradiction stems from within the voice of conscience utters truths.

Notes

Tarot Trump XVII illustrates very well the formative processes of creation. The appearance of Mars in the Path of this trump introduces an element of destructive force into the proceedings, and the conflict of interests is too great to pass without incident. The result is a failure to achieve any kind of stable alliance between the components involved. The fire of Mars sears and scorches the air of Aquarius, instead of merely warming it into useful activity.

6 in 12

Correspondences
Tiphareth, 'Beauty'; Sol. The Zodiacal Sign of Pisces, the Fishes; Tarot Trump XVIII 'The Moon'.

Sol rules the element Air; Pisces is of Water.

Main Principle   Sol in Atu XVIII 'The Moon'.

The Title   Light into darkness.

The Reading

Deep gulfs appear each side of the seeker on this Path. Diligence and precision of movement is required if one is not to fall.

Illusions well up from dark places to beguile the unwary; corruption manifests itself as beauty and charm. Attraction towards such illusion leads one into danger; shadows gather and take monstrous form.

Here we observe the descent of light into darkness. The darkness is great and consumes the light.

Thus the lower raises its blasphemous head in victory over the higher; hell-hounds bay from horizon to horizon. When the light of aspiration plunges lost into abominable places, the outcome will be the emergence of demons.

Good intent has become misplaced and distorted through ignorance of surrounding danger. The desire to create beneficial change has resulted in grief.

Progress cannot be achieved on the Path unless each step is taken in the all-penetrating light of wisdom. Thus the seeker who attains is he who looks to the goal with firm and rigid intent, knowing that in all deviation there lurks the demon Failure.

Notes

The integrating powers of Sol are drowned in the rank waters of Tarot Trump XVIII. This card is one of the least pleasant in the pack, unless modified by the presence of other more positive factors. But here the treachery of the card rules without sway; it is the victory of deception and corruption over all else. The light of Sol is absorbed by this foul Moon; it is the hag Hecate devouring the seed as it struggles to germinate.

The demons referred to in the reading should not be interpreted as actual personifications of 'evil' but as instances of unbalanced and potentially destructive events.

7 in 1

Correspondences
Netzach, 'Victory'; Venus. The Zodiacal Sign of Aries, the Ram; Tarot Trump IV 'The Emperor'.
 Venus rules the element Fire; Aries is of Fire.

Main Principle   Venus in Atu IV 'The Emperor'.

The Title   Downward flight.

The Reading

The Emperor who must make a judgement is a man who walks a tightrope; proper assessment and balanced action will result in a happy passage. Careless movement based on misconception will result in disaster.

The wise Emperor knows the foundation of all right judgement and deed. Why then, has he behaved as a fool?

The fool is he who makes decisions based only on the ruling of his heart; there is no assistance from objective reasoning to stem his downward flight. Only those who have trained their heart to mirror the divine balance of the Universe may act on such impulse and succeed. Such mortals are few.

Those who have achieved knowledge of divine balance may appear remote, even cruel, in the eyes of their fellow man, for their judgements are the hard judgements of Nature itself, which stoops not to consider the desires of mankind.

Therefore the Emperor who has abandoned the principles of true judgement for the sake of his heart has not judged well. He has fallen, and his judgement will be revealed as a sacrifice of wisdom for the sake of glamour.

Those whom the Emperor wished to impress will be the loudest in condemnation of his deed.

The Emperor, being in a position of authority, is yet able to reverse and correct his folly. He need not fear retribution; the peoples of his Empire would rather a hard and just man upon the throne steer them well, than a compassionate weakling lead them to disaster.

Notes

The Emperor, being aligned with the Cardinal Sign of Aries, represents an unstable force on the way to achieving stability. The somewhat cloying energies of Venus are not able to be properly transformed into useful channels of expression by one so essentially changeable. Firm and steady control is called for if any kind of success is to be achieved.

---

8 in 2

Correspondences
Hod, 'Glory'; Mercury. The Zodiacal Sign of Taurus, the Bull; Tarot Trump V 'The Hierophant'.
　　Mercury rules the element Water; Taurus is of Earth.

Main Principle　　Mercury in Atu V 'The Hierophant'.

The Title　　Dramatic change.

The Reading

One who has achieved the high status of Hierophant proceeds with the measured care attendant to wisdom. The cautious discharge of duties leads to worthy endeavour and lasting achievement.

The Hierophant's disciples benefit from such controlled mastery; they follow their leader in his footsteps and gain by example. The raising up of students to the higher levels of achievement cannot be accomplished without time and perseverance.

But here we observe the Hierophant who has received sudden illumination of great brilliance. He stands in the presence of knowledge that reveals superior means of attainment. Change must come quickly in the halls of learning; the disciples must be lead in new directions.

The old ways are dismissed in the light of the superior means; the announcing of such dramatic change may lead to anxiety and concern by those accustomed to tradition.

The Hierophant must now move with authority, exerting his influence over those in his charge and dispelling their confusion and anxiety. Speed in the pursuit of a worthy goal is not in itself deleterious if that speed is governed by wisdom. One who has received illumination is competent to seize advantage and act in haste without falling prey to error. The swift pursuit of superior means to attainment cannot be condemned, and justifies the shedding of obsolete practices.

Notes

Mercury entering the Path of Tarot Trump V produces sudden change in that which is normally slow to react. It is a perfect example of lightning striking the ground; it is the bolt from the blue that shakes everyone from their lethargy. As messenger of the gods, Mercury is a welcome visitor to the Hierophant, and indicates actions and decisions taken in the light of sound knowledge.

---

9 in 3

Correspondences
Yesod, 'Foundation'; Luna. The Zodiacal Sign of Gemini, the Twins; Tarot Trump VI 'The Lovers'.
  Luna rules the element Air; Gemini is of Air.

Main Principle: Luna in Atu VI 'The Lovers'.

The Title: Unfulfilled desire.

The Reading

To maintain a state of harmony the Lovers must have a consistent bond of mutual attraction. If that bond is disturbed a disruption of the processes creating harmony is inevitable. The maintenance of harmony requires the diligent application of wise and balanced conduct.

  Here we observe the disruption of harmony. Disturbance leads to a drawing apart; there is division where unity was desired. The Lovers proceed each to their own way.

  When unity is desired but division arises we see inconsistency between objective and achievement. There is no diligent application of wise and balanced conduct, merely the faint hope of wandering intention.

  A well-intentioned act executed in ignorance may turn anticipated pleasure into grief. The existence of division is a cause for grief when unity is desired; the loss of unity is replaced with no worthy substitute.

  If unfulfilled desire is to find its salvation the means of renewing harmony must be speedily established. Misplaced intention is in itself an error of no great magnitude; sincere efforts to make good the failings of ignorance will meet with favourable issue.

Notes

The airy nature of Luna cannot possibly assist the airy Sign of Gemini. Air is sterile and in full flow (as when Air meets Air) serves to erode rather than create. An abrasive element is the last requirement of Tarot Trump VI.

The Querent should not, of course, place too literal an interpretation on the use of the word 'Lovers' in the text; the reference is to two separate entities of any form seeking union.

---

3 in 4

Correspondences
Binah, 'Understanding'; Saturn. The Zodiacal Sign of Cancer, the Crab; Tarot Trump VII 'The Chariot'.

Saturn rules the element Water; Cancer is of Water.

Main Principle   Saturn in Tarot Trump VII 'The Chariot'.

The Title   Sorrow of departure.

The Reading

It is a time of sadness and joy for the Charioteer. His warrior's nature will provide him with the strength necessary to cope with such opposite emotions.

The Charioteer must leave his familiar land to travel the roads of his destiny. Only matters of great importance would lead those in high authority to dispatch their Charioteer upon this mission. Therefore, we are observing the actions of urgent necessity.

To leave behind the known and familiar to tread the unknown is often a cause for sorrow. Where the intended journey promises high reward the sorrow of departure is tempered by the joy of pleasurable anticipation. But where the journey is a descent from the higher to the lower, the sorrow of departure can not be overcome with ease.

Here we observe the Charioteer descending from the higher to the lower. His Path leads not to the illuminated summit, but to the darker realms below.

It is the duty of the Charioteer to obey those to whom he has freely pledged his services, therefore he will not doubt the necessity of his journey. And being possessed of the spirit of a warrior, the Charioteer will not succumb to sorrow but rise to joy, for he will be eager to employ his skills in the engagement of forthcoming obstacles. His joy will be the joy of challenge; his reward the exhilaration arising from successful endeavour.

Notes

Saturn occupies the Sephiroth from which the Charioteer of Tarot Trump VII descends on his way to Geburah. Thus the trump signifies the influence of Understanding descending on Strength. Here we see the waters of Cancer pouring down from their heights, where they have bathed in the light of the highest. It is part of the process of formation. One day that process will reverse; indeed it is the Charioteer's quest to encourage that reversal. The speed with which success is obtained is entirely dependent upon the efforts of the Charioteer.

---

4 in 5

Correspondences
Chesed, 'Mercy'; Jupiter. The Zodiacal Sign of Leo, the Lion; Tarot Trump XI 'Lust'.
   Jupiter rules the element Water; Leo is of Fire.

Main Principle   Jupiter in Atu XI 'Lust'.

The Title   Welcome fruit.

The Reading

The naked woman sits astride the mighty lion. Together they advance upon their journey with justifiable pride.

   The apparently weak and the manifestly strong are united in a harmonious association. The journey upon which they are engaged brings great benefit through experience.

   The naked woman is not vulnerable but secure; the mighty lion moves steadily under intelligent control. Coordinated effort overcomes all resistance. Useful lessons have been learned in the process of advancing.

The mighty lion is a kingly beast; the naked woman is eminently desirable. Together the woman and the lion are the image of nobility; they stand apart from all else. Thus they are distinct in their majesty. Such nobility secures the centre of attraction and diminishes criticism.

The desirable and the strong proceed together, and in their journeying win joy and reward. The wheel of fortune is turned in their favour; they enter a time of great prosperity. The lessons learned in the process of advancing are soon to bear welcome fruit.

The woman and the lion chose to unite and enter upon a telling quest; their innate nobility served to triumph over opposition. Those who are noble and approach prosperity through endeavour may justifiably advance with pride.

Notes

Tarot Trump XI spans the Path on the Tree of Life between the spheres of Strength and Mercy. The former is volatile, the latter stable. It is towards stability that events are now seen to proceed with a corresponding decrease in the instability of things volatile. The overall effect is an increase in all the benefits bestowed by Jupiter.

---

5 in 6

Correspondences
Geburah, 'Strength'; Mars. The Zodiacal Sign of Virgo, the Virgin; Tarot Trump IX 'The Hermit'. Mars rules the element Fire; Virgo is of Earth.

Main Principle   Mars in Atu IX 'The Hermit'.

The Title   Circle of despair.

The Reading

When the Hermit seeks attainment through entering the hermitage, he must be willing to accept the truths revealed to him through his long contemplations. The knowledge of truth serves no useful purpose if that knowledge is not rightfully employed. Truth can be unpalatable to one with immovable conceptions of what is acceptable.

The lessons of the hermitage bring fresh insights into the nature of Self. To receive new knowledge and reject it without due consideration is a folly; to dismiss truth in the protection of illusion and vanity is an even greater folly. The voice of the Self is soft, and will not be heard over the brayings of ignorance.

Here we observe the Hermit who has entered the hermitage, but he will not acknowledge the whisperings from within.

The world without responds to the world within; stubborness gives rise to needless obstructions. The hermit will enter a circle of despair: he will be angry at the nature of his knowledge, his anger will destroy the tranquility he seeks. In seeking tranquility he will enter despair; despair will lead to a search for tranquility.

By admitting to what is apparent, and acknowledging the realities of capacity and ability, the Hermit can create a world in tune with his needs. Happiness will then reign. Pursuit of what is false or beyond achievement can only bring misery.

Notes

The furious fires of Mars cannot bring any benefit to the Hermit of Tarot Trump IX: an aggressive quality or nature is out of place in such mystical company. Nor does the masculine aspect of Mars marry well with the earthy, feminine quality of Virgo. The grounds for future harmony, progress and fruition are not laid in arrogant and brash strokes, but through cooperative and placid endeavour.

---

6 in 7

Correspondences
Tiphareth, 'Beauty'; Sol. The Zodiacal Sign of Libra, the Balances; Tarot Trump VIII 'Adjustment'.

Sol rules the element Air; Libra is of Air.

Main Principle   Sol in Atu VIII 'Adjustment'.

The Title   Equity and virtue.

The Reading

Here we observe the coming together of things with measured grace. All tension and discontent departs in the harmonious union of compatible forces. It is as the gathering together and uniting of good friends who approach from all quarters near and far.

The convergence of such fellowship brings great happiness and satisfaction. It is a time for participating in new alliances, for establishing new plans and increasing resources.

The coming together of things with measured grace denotes that events have been organised with due regard for what is agreeable and just. Equity and virtue prohibits dissent; gatherings may take place in legitimate pleasure. Social intercourse furthers pleasure and disseminates useful knowledge.

Just and intelligent actions bring progress and advancement. Faith is vested in those who demonstrate virtuous conduct.

By selecting that which is desirable and casting out what is not, by taking up worthy incentives and pursuing just causes, the present direction will lead to stable and satisfying progress.

Notes

Sol and the Sephirah Tiphareth are located centrally on the Tree of Life; they are the focal point of the entire Tree and mediate between all extremes. It is therefore beneficial for Sol's influence to radiate within the Path of Tarot Trump VIII because this Trump represents the essence of balanced action. The result is one of reinforced equilibrium; events reach a stage of almost perfect harmony.

---

7 in 8

Correspondences
Netzach, 'Victory'; Venus. The Zodiacal Sign of Scorpio, the Scorpion; Tarot Trump XIII 'Death'.

Venus rules the element Fire; Scorpio is of Water.

Main Principle   Venus in Atu XIII 'Death'.

The Title   Gathering in of what is due.

The Reading

The duty of the reaper is to secure the harvest at the proper time and in the correct manner. Delay will result in a harvest over-ripe, whereas premature action will swiftly destroy rising potential. Even action taken at the proper time is worthless if the harvest is ruined through negligent handling.

When the reaper dutifully follows the demands of his calling he will achieve success and gain valuable reward for his labours. Should the reaper fail in the honourable discharge of his duties he will be surrounded by the contemptible yield of his deeds.

He who wields the scythe must know when and how to strike. A foolish act will reap nought but sorrow and cause for regret.

Here we observe the reaper who delays that which needs to be done. He is reluctant to wield his scythe and gather in the harvest of his planting. There will be no worthy achievement.

The reaper must understand that all things ripen at their appointed hour. The refusal to acknowledge the inevitable does not dismiss its presence. The gathering in of what is due can not be delayed beyond the limits of destiny's intention.

If the reaper desires to maintain the respect of his society he will gather in what is ripe and present it for inspection. Failure to fulfill the obligations of his calling will result in the loss of his position.

Notes

Tarot Trump XIII occupies the Path between Tiphareth and Netzach, the former being referred to Sol and the latter to Venus. The voluptuous nature of Venus here serves to prevent advance along the Path to the higher aspected Sol. It is the morning star blocking the greater light of day, the failure to accept responsibility for, and the consequences of, one's deeds. The covert suggestion is to 'stand up and be counted'.

---

8 in 9

Correspondences
Hod, 'Glory'; Mercury. The Zodiacal Sign of Sagittarius, the Archer; Tarot Trump XIV 'Art'.

Mercury rules the element Water; Sagittarius is of Fire.

Main Principle   Mercury in Atu XIV 'Art'.

The Title   Careless regard.

101

The Reading

The fulfilment of aspiration requires the application of practical effort. The organisation of things useful to progress can not be accomplished in the absence of forethought, nor will impractical schemes enlist the aid of wise and able helpers.

Here we observe one who aspires to a worthy goal yet proceeds with careless regard for the means of achievement. Plans are evolved which bear no relation to what is possible or desirable. It is as the archer who, in desiring to strike his mark, measures the winds and distances yet possesses neither bow nor arrow equal to the task.

Aspiration is fulfilled when observation reaches out and encompasses all things relevant to progress. Thoughtful consideration of what is possible and desirable will encourage and enhance progress. Wise and able helpers will readily aid the pursuit of practical and worthy ambition.

The pursuit of the impractical will lead to regret and the loss both of time and acquaintances. Stubborn advance under such conditions will bring retaliation swift on the heels of grief.

Notes

Tarot Trump XIV occupies the vertically aspected Path between Tiphareth and Yesod. The appearance of Mercury suggests deviation from the vertical, i.e. that progress has been temporarily deflected – probably through no deliberate intention – and that events must be brought back into line. It is a question of seeking the appropriate balance between extremes.

---

9 in 10

Correspondences

Yesod, 'Foundation'; Luna. The Zodiacal Sign of Capricorn, the Goat; Tarot Trump XV 'The Devil'.

Luna rules the element Air, Capricorn is of Earth.

Main Principle   Luna in Atu XV 'The Devil'.

The Title   The Company of danger.

The Reading

Progress on the Path, as through life itself, is assisted by knowledge of the propriety of each successive step.

The wild mountain goat, in ascending the difficult and hazardous slopes to the high summit, ensures that every foothold is firm and secure. Instinct and observation serve to aid the ascent and achieve favourable issue.

Man alone upon the earth is possessed of a mighty intellect. When progress is seen to decline when ascent is desired, the traveller, for all his superior intellect, is not the equal of the beast upon a rocky slope.

Here we observe one who is ascending without proper regard for hazards. The footholds are not firm but prone to sudden collapse. Nor is the way ahead clear, but hidden in obscuring shadow. The traveller therefore proceeds in the company of danger.

Further advance should not be attempted until the way ahead is without shadow, nor until the footholds can be gauged for firmness.

Forced progress under such adverse conditions will surely lead to grief. Even noble aspiration cannot excuse such folly. Determination to pursue a course through unsafe surroundings will only yield success when the traveller is at ease in the midst of peril.

Notes

The blustery, airy nature of Luna serves to erode the earth of Capricorn, scattering the element in all directions. Stability is thus undermined. This is reflected in the effect upon Tarot Trump XV; the forces of generation are inverted and become almost self-destructive. This can possibly be attributed to Luna's habit of deception, through the tendency to produce illusions in the half-light of her radiance. It is the pursuit of a false or unworthy goal.

---

3 in 11

Correspondences
Binah, 'Understanding'; Saturn. The Zodiacal Sign of Aquarius, the Water-bearer; Tarot Trump XVII 'The Star'.

Saturn rules the element Water; Aquarius is of Air.

Main Principle   Saturn in Atu XVII 'The Star'.

The Title   Movement and growth.

The Reading

A star pours down its welcome light upon a darkened world. Still waters respond to the light from above; motion occurs in the deeps.

When starlight falls upon darkness and the still is given motion, it is the voice of the Self issuing from the higher, and the world of the lower rising in response. What was stagnant is given motion and direction, what was cold and dark is warmed and made light. Change now comes in accordance with the needs of Self.

Movement and growth will occur in a measured and regulated manner. Careful activity will yield advantage and the establishment of long enduring works. The laws of the Universe are not broken, therefore that which now comes is both lawful and agreeable.

When motion occurs in the deeps we see also a rising up of latent forces. New energy comes into being to spur the fires of aspiration and deed. This leads to great and worthy creativity, and brings the rewards of successful endeavour.

Illumination from above reveals hidden obstruction; the Path ahead is made clear and can be journeyed without danger. Advancing in the company of lawful authority disperses unlawful resistance; great creativity enhances the joy of untroubled advance.

Notes

Saturn in the Path of Tarot Trump XVII serves to bring order and control to the processes of creativity. This suggests careful planning and the formation of enduring works. It is the disciplined canvas of the professional artist, as compared with the undisciplined dabbling of the careless amateur. It is 'La Gioconda' compared with meaningless abstracts.

It is self-evident that careful planning and discipline of this order results in success.

---

4 in 12

Correspondences
Chesed, 'Mercy'; Jupiter. The Zodiacal Sign of Pisces, the Fishes; Tarot Trump XVIII 'The Moon'.

Jupiter rules the element Water; Pisces is of Water.

Main Principle   Jupiter in Atu XVIII 'The Moon'.

The Title   Exhaustion.

The Reading

When great efforts are made to secure progress in the wrong direction, the outcome will be grief.

One should not seek to advance unless the intended Path is seen to be worthy. Ignorance of what lies ahead points to danger. No matter how well-intentioned the deed, all action undertaken in ignorance leaves one prey to misfortune.

Here we observe the wasteful expenditure of considerable resources. Admirable intention is enmeshed in folly. The forces of growth are dissipated in the treacherous contortions of dark places. The result is exhaustion. An unworthy Path thus claims one who has not balanced intention with provident care.

Considerable resources are only acquired through careful husbandry; they indicate the presence of keen intelligence. One who possesses keen intelligence will quickly observe the effects of depletion, and withdraw before all is exhausted and lost. In this way complete disaster is avoided; the means will exist to start anew.

A useful lesson will be gained from such an experience. Ambition and intention will be tempered with increased foresight; future actions will reflect the lessons of the past.

Having once encountered dark and unworthy places, the wise man resolves to avoid a repetition of such folly, and redoubles his efforts to employ his valuable resources to useful ends.

Notes

Jupiter rules the Sign of Pisces, but even this does not fully insulate the positive nature of Jupiter against the negative forces of the corresponding Tarot Trump. Atu XVIII 'The Moon' is one of the least auspicious in the pack; it effectively represents unpleasant conditions. Only the innate strength of Jupiter enables entrance and exit to be made from these conditions without the gravest penalties being incurred. Thus great strength is seen to overcome danger.

5 in 1

Correspondences
Geburah, 'Strength'; Mars. The Zodiacal Sign of Aries, the Ram; Tarot Trump IV 'The Emperor'.

Mars rules the element Fire; Aries is of Fire.

Main Principle   Mars in Atu IV 'The Emperor'.

The Title   Victorious.

The Reading

When the Emperor has taken on his armour and his lance, it is clear that words are of no further use.

If diplomacy has failed and the Empire is threatened, the Emperor has taken the proper course by making preparations for combat. If diplomacy has not been exhausted, or if the Empire is not under threat, there will be nothing to gain from an aggressive advance.

But the Emperor has already taken on his armour and his lance is raised, therefore we observe the unmistakeable gestures of his intention.

The Emperor in a warrior's stance strikes fear into those who would oppose him. This will encourage the opposition to withdraw. No confrontation will take place. Success will be achieved without struggle.

Should the opposition choose not to withdraw but to remain, the Emperor will succeed over them. But there will be casualties numbered on both sides.

Thus we see the Emperor victorious as the inevitable outcome of his present stance. He will overcome all resistance.

If deeds alone can secure the day, the Emperor has taken the proper course. If words have still their part to complete, victory will be hollow after conquest.

Notes

The entrance of fiery Mars into the Path of Tarot Trump IV cannot but produce a grand conflagration. The corresponding Sign of Aries is Cardinal; its fires are newborn, fierce and unstable. When Mars enters Aries and adds flame to flame the resultant force is sufficient to overcome everything in its presence. However, great care must be exercised when handling such energy.

6 in 2

Correspondences
Tiphareth, 'Beauty'; Sol. The Zodiacal Sign of Taurus, the Bull; Tarot Trump V 'The Hierophant'.

Sol rules the element Air; Taurus is of Earth.

Main Principle   Sol in Atu V 'The Hierophant'.

The Title   Self-indulgence.

The Reading

The Hierophant is he who listens to the voice deep within and opens his mind to the helpful influences from above. Thus he journeys successfully from the lower to the higher Paths.

The life of the Hierophant is therefore one of constant exploration and discovery, a pressing forward from the kingdom of the known into the realm of the unknown.

When pressing forward is of such vital importance a journeying into self-indulgence will bring no advance. There will be a decline into folly and grief.

Self-indulgence is a great and cunning adversary, presenting itself in many deceiving guises. When the future looms vacant or cold it is a great comfort to cling to the anchors of the past. By holding on to what is known the ever-coming future is robbed of its victory. This is self-indulgence. The holding on to what is known cannot bring progress.

Worthy progress is achieved when existing resources are combined into a useful weapon, and employed in the steady advance upon the future. The future is not then the victor but the vanquished. But even the pursuit of unobtainable goals is an indulgence when success is seen to be beyond reach.

The Hierophant listens to the voice deep within and acknowledges the virtue of honesty.

Notes

Sol normally indicates the functions of integration, coordination and synthesis, processes which ought to result in progress. But here we see how Sol serves to hold back the Hierophant of Tarot Trump V, for the earth of the corresponding Sign of Taurus cannot respond to the airy Sol; there is no positive to negative interplay, no mixing of complementary factors necessary if gestation is to occur. In short, the motive force for growth is absent.

7 in 3

Correspondences
Netzach, 'Victory'; Venus. The Zodiacal Sign of Gemini, the Twins; Tarot Trump VI 'The Lovers'.

Venus rules the element Fire; Gemini is of Air.

Main Principle　Venus in Atu VI 'The Lovers'.

The Title　Absence of calm.

The Reading

Though the Lovers desire to unite and become as one, they may yet frustrate intention by their very own deeds.

Progress towards the achievement of harmony and satisfaction is made possible when objectives are pursued with wise and balanced conduct. The approach of an objective after much endeavour often leads to great excitement. The absence of calm permits the entrance of error. Thus the final stages in the journey towards achievement are beset with dangers; the excitement of anticipated victory may lead to the premature withdrawal of caution.

Obstacles are then encountered unexpectedly. They rise up as great barriers through the want of advance preparation.

If the two would unite and become as one the process of coming together must allow for the unexpected appearance of obstacles until the last. Too abandoned an approach will lead to later difficulty.

By proceeding with wise and balanced conduct, neither modifying pace nor advancing without caution, the Lovers will secure their union without undue delay or regret. The excitement of conquest should not be given free reign until the victory has been won.

Notes

The Lovers are of a somewhat volatile nature and are prone to sudden change. The fiery nature of Venus entering the airy Sign of Gemini effects unwelcome change, for Tarot Trump VI then represents one swamped in idealism rather than clear perception. It is as though the fires of Venus expand the Air of Gemini in all directions, instead of concentrating it to a point. The result is a tendency to overlook the hard and vital facts of life.

8 in 4

Correspondences
Hod, 'Glory'; Mercury. The Zodiacal Sign of Cancer, the Crab; Tarot Trump VII 'The Chariot'.

Mercury rules the element Water; Cancer is of Water.

Main Principle   Mercury in Atu VII 'The Chariot'.

The Title   Speed and distinction.

The Reading

Unless the Charioteer is adept in the control of his craft the swiftest steeds and the finest chariot will not serve to secure victory.

Success is achieved when all the composite elements function in harmony through skilful control. The greatest success of all is achieved through the expert command of an outstanding chariot and team.

Here we observe a magnificent chariot advancing at lightning speed. The Charioteer stands firmly as a proud warrior at the reins; the galloping steeds breathe flame in the passion of their flight. All the elements are in their rightful place; all things converge in harmonious purpose. Achievement and success are forthcoming.

Whether the Charioteer speeds onward for the sake of sport or war is of no consequence. Such mastery must have its own victory.

When the chariot proceeds with such swiftness the Charioteer does not contemplate matters beyond those of immediate consequence. All thought and action must be concentrated to a point. Progress is made through the unswerving will to succeed. Intelligence and skill combine to snatch advantage from the onrushing flow of opportunity. The Charioteer enlists the aid of all useful and superior resources to assist him in his quest.

Clearly the Charioteer is a master of his art. One who advances with such speed and distinction will not be dismayed if those of lesser ability are indignant at his success.

Notes

Cancer is a Cardinal Sign of the element Water and, as such, lacks the quality of stability. This is reflected in part in the corresponding Tarot trump, which is a vision of inspired motion. Where motion exists nothing but change itself is guaranteed. The entrance of Mercury indicates matters proceeding at a spanking pace, with great precision and economy of means. The drawback, if drawback it is, is that Mercury is wholly cold blooded and ruthless. These qualities will possibly be apparent throughout the forthcoming sequence of events.

---

9 in 5

Correspondences
Yesod, 'Foundation'; Luna. The Zodiacal Sign of Leo, the Lion; Tarot Trump XI 'Lust'.

Luna rules the element Air; Leo is of Fire.

Main Principle   Luna in Atu XI 'Lust'.

The Title   Over-confidence.

The Reading

Peaceful collaboration between two companions is maintained when differences are ignored for the sake of mutual interests. When forces join together to pursue one ambition the goal is speedily met. But when one companion seeks dominance, or draws apart to follow a lone indulgence, the partnership will dissolve and even minor differences become exaggerated. This leads to enmity and regret.

Here we observe the woman who rides upon a lion, and who falls prey to over-confidence. Imagining herself more powerful and cunning than the beast itself, she foolishly runs the risk of incurring its wrath. There will be discord where once was acceptance and trust.

Valuable companionship is placed in grave jeopardy. The weak imagines itself strong and exerts false authority. The strong senses the coming of folly, and feels its helpful submission abused.

The lion will rise up and snap the reins that bind strength and weakness in peaceful coexistence. The lion will stride on; the woman will fall and be abandoned without company or comfort.

The fallen rider will not successfully encourage another lion to accept her presence until her illusions of greatness have passed. In her loneliness she will curse the folly of her ways, and regret the loss of a valuable companion.

Notes

Tarot Trump XI occupies the Path on the Tree of Life between Chesed,

Mercy, and Geburah, Strength. There is obviously a need for fine balance when bridging two such elements. The entrance of Luna into that fine balance serves to inflate certain aspects represented by the trump. The airy part of Luna is attempting to overwhelm the fiery part of Leo. The result is overbalance and separation.

---

3 in 6

Correspondences
Binah, 'Understanding'; Saturn. The Zodiacal Sign of Virgo, the Virgin; Tarot Trump IX 'The Hermit'.
  Saturn rules the element Water, Virgo is of Earth.

Main Principle   Saturn in Atu IX 'The Hermit'.

The Title   Process of decay.

The Reading
Here we observe the slow and methodical bearing down on the withdrawn and contemplative. From this we see the emergence of misdirected activity.

When the slow and methodical brings its forces to bear on the withdrawn and contemplative, we see that which is already subdued and inactive becoming bound in the ties of needless anxiety. Great attention is given to that which deserves but little. Time spent in the pursuit of minor affairs leads to the unhappy neglect of important matters.

The important then enters a period of decline; minor affairs detract from worthy duties but yield no benefit. It is as the Hermit who, being shut up in his cell, spends his time in the contemplation of the mysteries of fable, while ignoring the greater realities that reside in his heart.

Such behaviour will not bring progress. Rather it will speed the process of decay.

Progress comes when the important is granted the attention it both deserves and requires. To sacrifice the important for the sake of minor affairs is a folly born of weakness. Strength and courage are required to face the mighty; minor affairs are despatched with ease.

111

Notes

The dark waters of Saturn flood the soil of Virgo; the potential of the Earth is lost under the onslaught. The Hermit of Tarot Trump IX is thus similarly afflicted; he is unable to break through to the surface and bathe in the true light. He remains instead a solitary figure, doubting and resisting the one means to his release. He is condemned to remain in isolation until he realizes the folly of his ways and opens himself up to assistance.

---

4 in 7

Correspondences
Chesed, 'Mercy'; Jupiter. The Zodiacal Sign of Libra, the Balances; Tarot Trump VIII 'Adjustment'.

Jupiter rules the element Water; Libra is of Air.

Main Principle   Jupiter in Atu VIII 'Adjustment'.

The Title   Sending forth and receiving.

The Reading

Here we observe the processes of sending forth and receiving. The left hand receives and the right hand gives, the right hand receives and the left hand gives. Thus there is balanced and agreeable action, but there is no true growth.

Resources are neither diminished nor increased, but exchanged and shared. What is of no further use to one is given to another and turned to advantage.

Such sharing does not increase wealth, but brings great happiness and establishes friendship. This leads to a greater contentment with life, and brings the benefits of increased prosperity when growth does not exist or is not possible.

Useful progress can be made at such a time. When contentment comes pleasure follows; this encourages the continuation of sharing and brings beneficial change into the community.

From beneficial change will grow true prosperity; the initial sharing of resources opens new opportunity, which can be used to create advantage by one who seeks to leave a circle of equality.

Notes

The expansive nature of Jupiter is somewhat modified by Tarot Trump VIII, which seeks to control an imbalance in one direction by compensating accordingly. Therefore, any advantage which Jupiter might bring is accompanied simultaneously by a calculated loss. But Jupiter represents a potent force. The process of compensating will inevitably yield to Jupiter's determination to dominate and true growth will then take place, as the final paragraph of the reading indicates.

---

5 in 8

Correspondences
Geburah, 'Strength'; Mars. The Zodiacal Sign of Scorpio, the Scorpion; Tarot Trump XIII 'Death'.

Mars rules the element Fire; Scorpio is of Water.

Main Principle Mars in Atu XIII 'Death'.

The Title Scything down.

The Reading

It is the function and duty of the reaper to cut down that which should no longer stand. In this way opposition to attainment on the Path is removed.

The Reaper who proceeds with reluctance, who is unwilling to cut down the apparently desirable, has failed to learn the lesson of necessity, neither has he any comprehension of truth.

The greatest obstacles to one who seeks progress are those outwardly beautiful, outwardly desirable. These qualities serve to hold the seeker in their presence, arresting progress by turning attention from its proper course. Necessity demands that all things arresting progress are removed. Truth reveals that all obstacles to progress are inwardly corrupt.

The Reaper who has learned the lesson of necessity and comprehends truth will advance steadily on the Path. He will not stay the action of his scythe.

Here we observe the Reaper who boldly and with great vigour sets about his task of scything down. There is no hesitation in his action. The obstructions to progress fall and are gone. Necessity and truth are his companions.

When boldness and vigour are displayed in the correct time and manner little resistance to progress is encountered. The weakness at the core of the inwardly corrupt serves to keep them subdued in the presence of the strong. The weak fear the strength of necessity and truth.

But the reaper must observe a measure of caution by ensuring that in his vigour he does not scythe down that which should stand, which is the very truth that guides and inspires him.

Notes

Mars is 5, the pentagram that invokes and banishes. Its fiery nature is well aspected in the Path of Tarot Trump XIII, where the warrior-like activity of scything down is implicit. We see the pentagram invoking Aspiration and banishing resistance; the Reaper advances with deadly strokes. It is an Omen of good fortune, indicating as it does great strength of purpose.

6 in 9

Correspondences
Tiphareth, 'Beauty'; Sol. The Zodiacal Sign of Sagittarius, the Archer; Tarot Trump XIV 'Art'.

Sol rules the element Air; Sagittarius is of Fire.

Main Principle   Sol in Atu XIV 'Art'.

The Title   Fruition of labours.

The Reading

Here we observe great and undeniable success. The Path has been traversed from the unstable and changing to the fixed and eternal. Darkness and light are no longer in contention. Illumination prevails over all. All shadows are diminished.

It is a time for the union of all desirable things, and for the departure of all things undesired.

Aspiration has guided willing hands; the building up and blending of useful and worthy elements into one balanced form has brought forth the reward of concerted and diligent effort.

Such success will lead to new opportunity along rewarding Paths. The crossroads have been reached, but all darkness lies to the rear and only joy and attainment lie ahead.

Assistance and companionship will approach from all quarters. It is a time for the expansion of horizons, and for the fruition of labours. Success will be accompanied by enthusiastic and encouraging acclaim.

By maintaining the levels of past conduct and aspiration the traveller will continue to ascend by the straight and true Path, neither deviating to the left or right, nor returning again to the unstable and changing.

Notes

Tarot Trump XIV occupies the 25th Path of the Tree of Life, between Tiphareth and Yesod, and is vertically situated on the Middle Pillar. It is in direct line with Kether, 'the Crown'. The process of Transformation represented by the Trump has therefore been successfully completed; the ascent to Tiphareth (as indicated by the appearance of Sol) marks a high level of attainment. Undeviating effort will lead to the very Crown itself.

---

7 in 10

Correspondences
Netzach, 'Victory'; Venus. The Zodiacal Sign of Capricorn, the Goat; Tarot Trump XV 'The Devil'.

Venus rules the element Fire; Capricorn is of Earth.

Main Principle   Venus in Atu XV 'The Devil'.

The Title   New works.

The Reading

The mountain of life soars ever aloft before the traveller on his journey. The relentless slope leads from the flatlands of hope to the high peak above, which glitters in the illumination from the heavens. The wise and strong of will abandon the lands of hope and take to the slopes that they may attain to the radiant light.

Desire burns within the breast of the traveller standing upon the slopes. One who thus embarks upon a journey will not waver on the upward way.

The traveller who ascends the Path burdened with premonitions of danger and toil will advance with heavy and reluctant steps. Such journeying will cloud the vision of all that is beheld at the ending of the way. But when one ascends with the joy and the vision of beauty that springs from desire, the summit will yield its fullest delight.

Great progress is now indicated. Unselfishness and firmness accompany the seeker and traveller. The desire to overcome inertia succeeds; creation takes the place of inactivity. It is a time for the establishment of new works. Unselfishness and firmness encourage the attraction of devoted companions; new works and companions flourish in the expression of desire.

Notes

The fires of Venus serve to inspire the earthy spirit of Capricorn; the mountain-goat ascends the slopes in a state of inspired rapture. The vision of beauty referred to in the reading is in a sense a vision of truth; from Netzach is observed the Sephirah Tiphareth which is the very heart of the Tree of Life. This may suggest that the Querent possesses already a sense of destiny, even though that destiny is, as yet, vague and unrealized.

8 in 11

Correspondences
Hod, 'Glory'; Mercury. The Zodiacal Sign of Aquarius, the Water-bearer; Tarot Trump XVII 'The Star'.
    Mercury rules the element Water; Aquarius is of Air.

Main Principle   Mercury in Atu XVII 'The Star'.

The Title   Responding to necessity.

The Reading

Here the forces of creativity reach down from the higher and fill the lower. Even the land and sea respond in agreeable activity. New growth occurs in every quarter; flowers rise up and blossom on the land, young fishes swim in deep waters. All things multiply and become many. Increase is established in its season.

The Universe is never still but ceaselessly exchanges growth and decay as it strives for perfection. All that occurs is therefore an act of necessity; all things are part of the Universal plan. When the forces of creativity give rise to agreeable activity we see the elements responding to necessity. There is no undue resistance to the pursuit of so noble an end; where need is present the Universe flows to fill that need. The result is satisfaction and increase.

Such activity is reflected in the world of man by deeds producing good fortune. Careful observation of need and the assessment of available resources will result in the formation of wise action. Attention to small detail, and the thoughtful consideration of every act, brings worthy benefits to the family and to one's society. The season of increase, when fully established, is not confined to individuals but is savoured by all who are in need.

When need is replaced by satisfaction the Universe has moved closer to the fulfilment of its grand design.

Notes

Mercury is the winged messenger of the gods and is further associated with the processes of constructive thought. When Mercury enters the Path of Tarot Trump XVII 'The Star' we see light from the latter duly modified and informed by the former. As it is the function of the Star to illumine the world of mortals in their darkness, it is self-evident that Mercury is beneficial in this process.

---

9 in 12

Correspondences
Yesod, 'Foundation'; Luna. The Zodiacal Sign of Pisces, the Fishes; Tarot Trump XVIII 'The Moon'.
    Luna rules the element Air, Pisces is of Water.

Main Principle   Luna in Atu XVIII 'The Moon'.

The Title   Folly.

The Reading

This is truly the Path of all illusion; deception abounds from horizon to horizon.

This is the darkest midnight, and the hour of the deepest shadow. The releasing dawn is yet far ahead; the twilight of evening has long receeded. There is no helpful light either above or below to guide the way ahead.

The Path leading directly from the lower to the higher has been lost. The seeker has strayed, and will flounder in the consequences of unfortunate folly. Rarely is such misfortune observed in the courses of the celestial tides.

The weakling succumbs under such dark oppression; the strong-willed survive by hastening to places of safety. To proceed in the face of such unwelcome resistance will result in sorrow.

The strong of will do not permit themselves to be overcome by the consequences of folly. By hastening to places of safety they are able to gather their resolve to succeed; this in itself is beneficial though small progress.

Still greater progress is made by seeking out the point of departure from the original and true Path. By understanding the root cause of deviation, further acts of folly are then avoided.

Notes

Tarot Trump XVIII is here the indicator of an unstable phase in one's life. When the negative forces of Luna are effectively doubled, as in this instance, the consequences can be disastrous. Luna here appears as the dark goddess Hecate, eager to leap forth and destroy.

But Luna is subject to constant and swift change; one phase follows and reverses the other. Darkness will give way to light. The reading indicates that sensible actions and precautions are likely to see one safely through. Yet if there is a choice, it is better not to proceed at all.

Appendix – Zodiacal Signs, Tarot Trumps and the Planets

Note that Tarot referred to throughout is that designed by Aleister Crowley (1845-1947).

The Zodiacal Signs and Tarot trumps

1 *Aries the Ram* Aries represents the desire to act in an energetic manner with a certain degree of aggressiveness and objectivity. The corresponding Tarot trump, Atu IV 'The Emperor' indicates vigour, aspiration, rule and conquest. Both occupy the 28th Path.

2 *Taurus the Bull* Taurus represents the desire to relate to the natural environment, a desire for solid security and material goods. The corresponding Tarot trump, Atu V 'The Hierophant' indicates the comfort of religion, stubborn strength, toil, wise counsel. Both occupy the 16th Path.

3 *Gemini the Twins* Gemini represents the desire to communicate one's thoughts to others, to adjust to circumstances and relate to the environment in general. The corresponding Tarot trump, Atu VI 'The Lovers' indicates the properties of intuition, intelligence and swift adaptability. Both occupy the 17th Path.

4 *Cancer the Crab* Cancer represents the desire to own, possess; to defend one's possessions and home. The corresponding Tarot trump, Atu VII 'The Chariot' indicates success through initiative, the surmounting of obstacles, victory through effort. Both occupy the 18th Path.

119

5 *Leo the Lion*   Leo represents the desire to obtain power, to achieve dominance. The corresponding Tarot trump, Atu XI 'Lust' indicates the reconciliation of opposing forces, the opportunity to advance, use of magical power, great courage. Both occupy the 19th Path.

6 *Virgo the Virgin*   Virgo represents the desire to achieve perfection, to be independent, efficient. The corresponding Tarot trump, Atu IX 'The Hermit' indicates a need for isolation or withdrawal, discretion, careful planning; also illumination from within. Both occupy the 20th Path.

7 *Libra the Balances*   Libra represents the desire to unite and relate with others, to obtain social order. The corresponding Tarot trump, Atu VIII 'Adjustment' indicates treaties, the formation of partnerships, marriage, negotiations, vindication of truth. Both occupy the 22nd Path.

8 *Scorpio the Scorpion*   Scorpio represents the desire to know the fundamental principles of life; to seek power, sex; to know one's Self. The corresponding Tarot trump, Atu XIII 'Death' indicates starting afresh, unexpected change, destruction. Both occupy the 24th Path.

9 *Sagittarius the Archer*   Sagittarius represents the desire to expand horizons, to seek freedom, to experiment. The corresponding Tarot trump, Atu XIV 'Art', indicates the joining of forces, harmonious partnerships, control of volatile situations, success. Both occupy the 25th Path.

10 *Capricorn the Goat*   Capricorn represents the desire to create order out of chaos, to submit to discipline, to become self-sufficient. The corresponding Tarot trump, Atu XV 'The Devil' indicates hidden forces at work, the need to transmute lower aspects of Being into useful energies; secret activities, unscrupulous methods. Both occupy the 26th Path.

11 *Aquarius the Water-bearer*   Aquarius represents the desire to transform one's society, to improve by modification, to identify with progressive trends. The corresponding Tarot trump, Atu XVII 'The Star' indicates the expansion of horizons, unexpected help, increased vigour, new outlook. Both occupy the 15th Path.

12 *Pisces the Fishes*   Pisces represents the desire to destroy barriers and restrictions, to transcend the material world, to examine established

norms. The corresponding Tarot trump, Atu XVIII 'The Moon' indicates illusion, deceit, a crisis of faith, the brink. Both occupy the 29th Path.

This completes the first sequence of symbols. The second concerns the seven planets. They are each designated with a numerical value as dictated by the Sephirah they occupy on the Tree of Life.

The Planets

3   Three refers to the Sephirah Binah, 'Understanding', and the planet Saturn. Saturn symbolises natural law, order and government, also restriction and decline in its negative aspect.

4   Four refers to the Sephirah Chesed, 'Mercy', and the planet Jupiter. Jupiter symbolises stability, growth, maturity and magnificence.

5   Five refers to the Sephirah Geburah, 'Strength', and the planet Mars. Mars symbolises energy, courage, cruelty, aggression and energetic expression.

6   Six refers to the Sephirah Tiphareth, 'Beauty', and our Sun, called Sol. Sol symbolises integration, balance, creative strength, harmony.

7   Seven refers to the Sephirah Netzach, 'Victory', and the planet Venus. Venus symbolises love and the lower associated emotions, also sympathy, sexual polarity.

8   Eight refers to the Sephirah Hod, 'Glory', and the planet Mercury. Mercury symbolises the intellect, logical thought, cunning, trickery, communication.

9   Nine refers to the Sephirah Yesod, 'Foundation', and our Moon, called Luna. Luna symbolises the subsconscious mind, rhythmic change, fluctuation, receptivity.

Index